COLOR

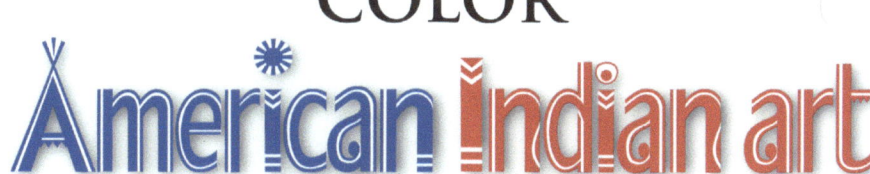
American Indian art

Conceived, Designed, and Illustrated by:

Mrinal Mitra

Series Edited by:

Swarna Mitra & **Malika Mitra**

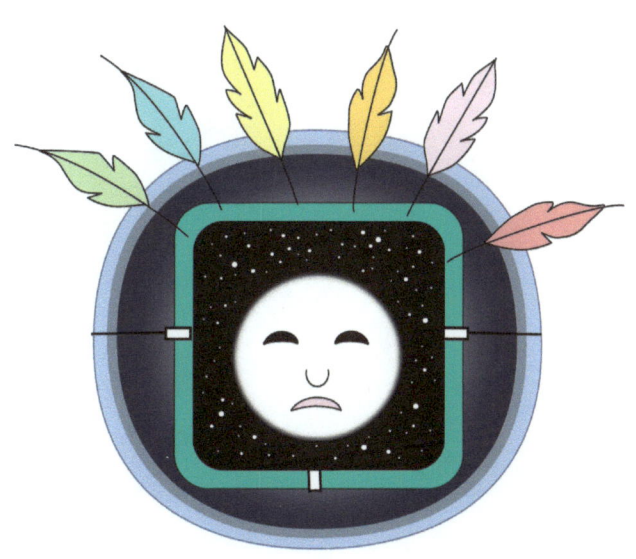

WORLD CULTURE COLORING SERIES

This series is dedicated to the citizens of the world;
from the young blooming minds of children, to the aspired individuals of all ages.

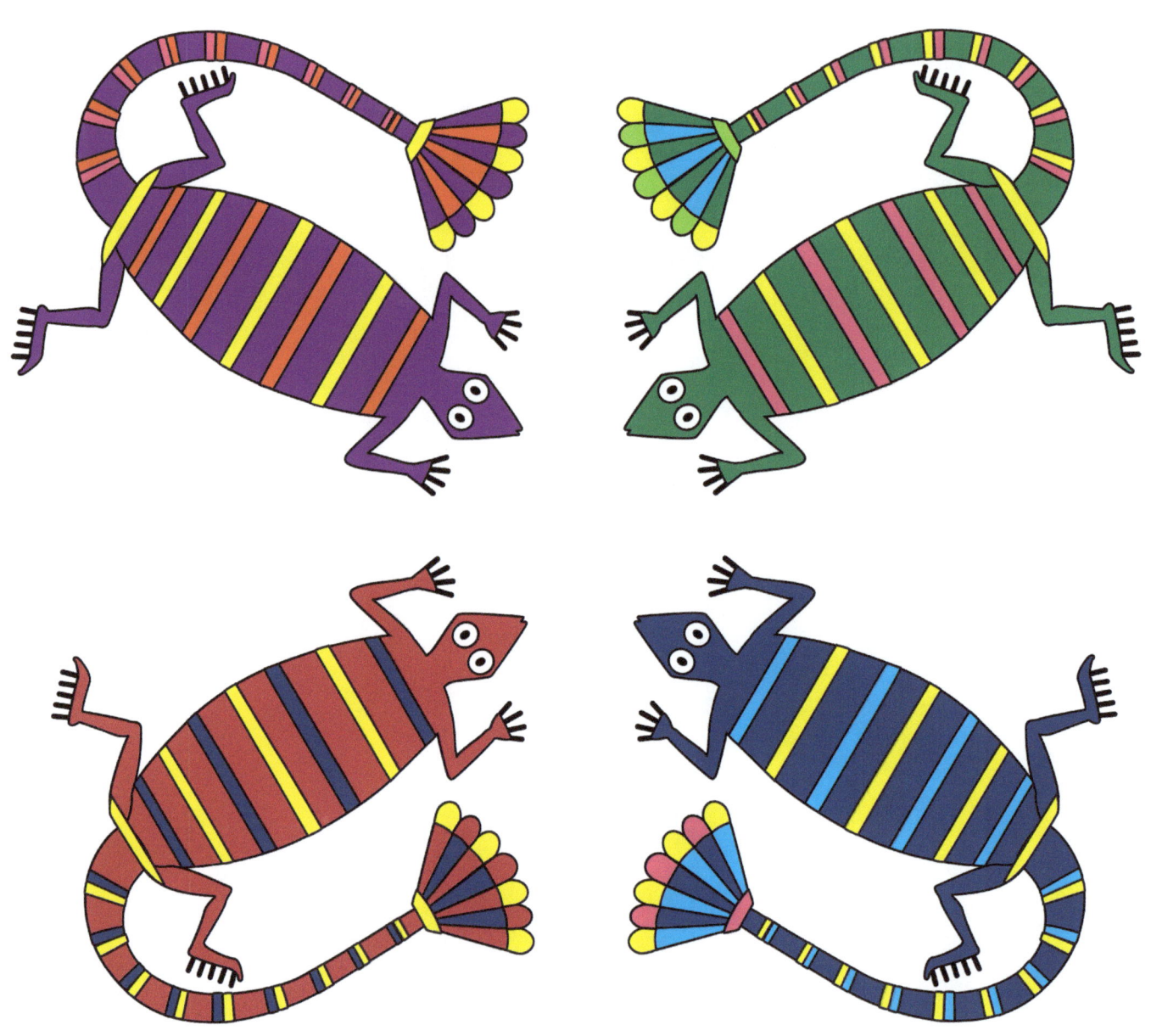

Mimbres figurative elements with geometric designs on the jar.
New Mexico, USA, 1981.

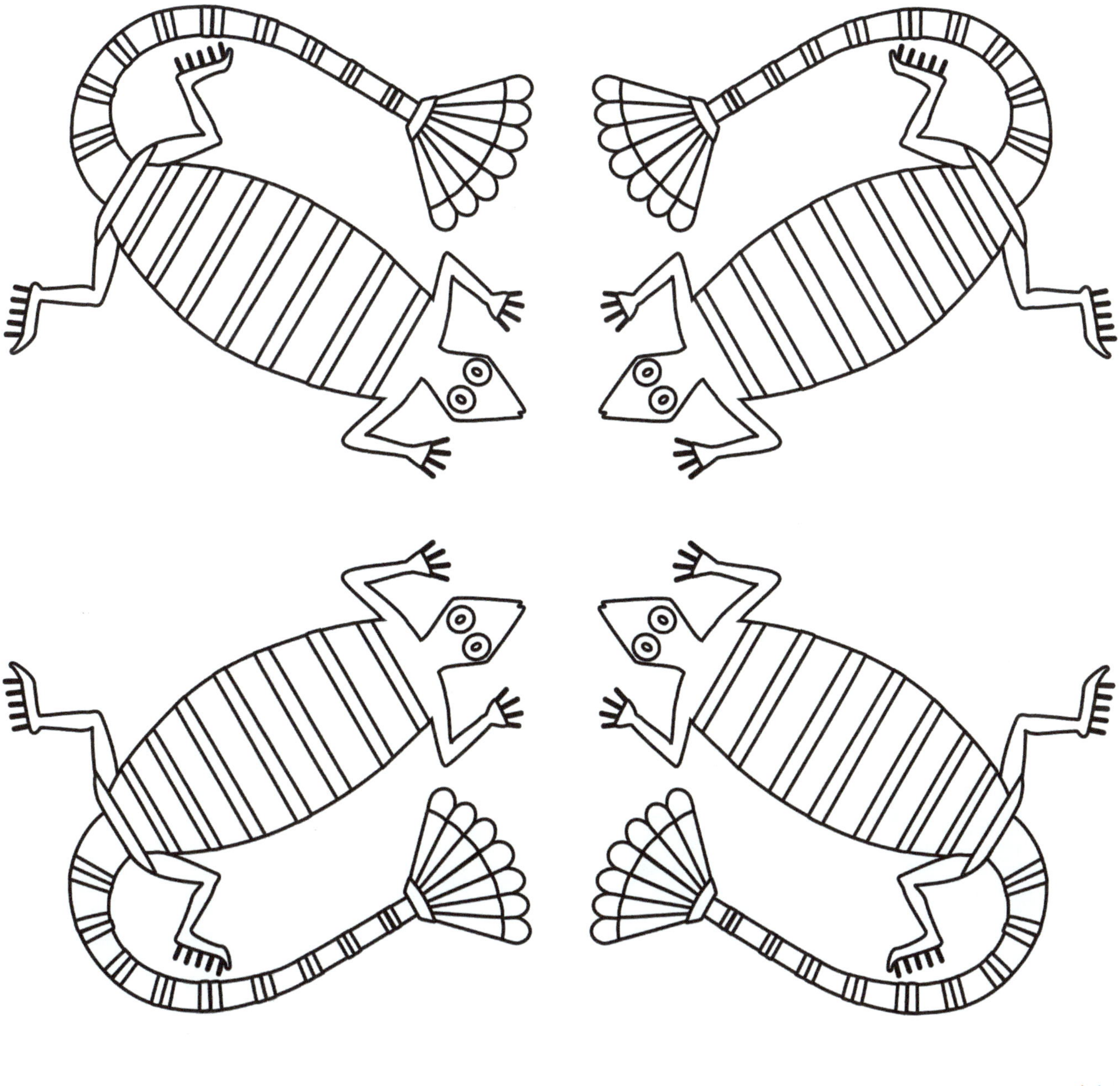

Color the drawings above using your preferred choice of colors.

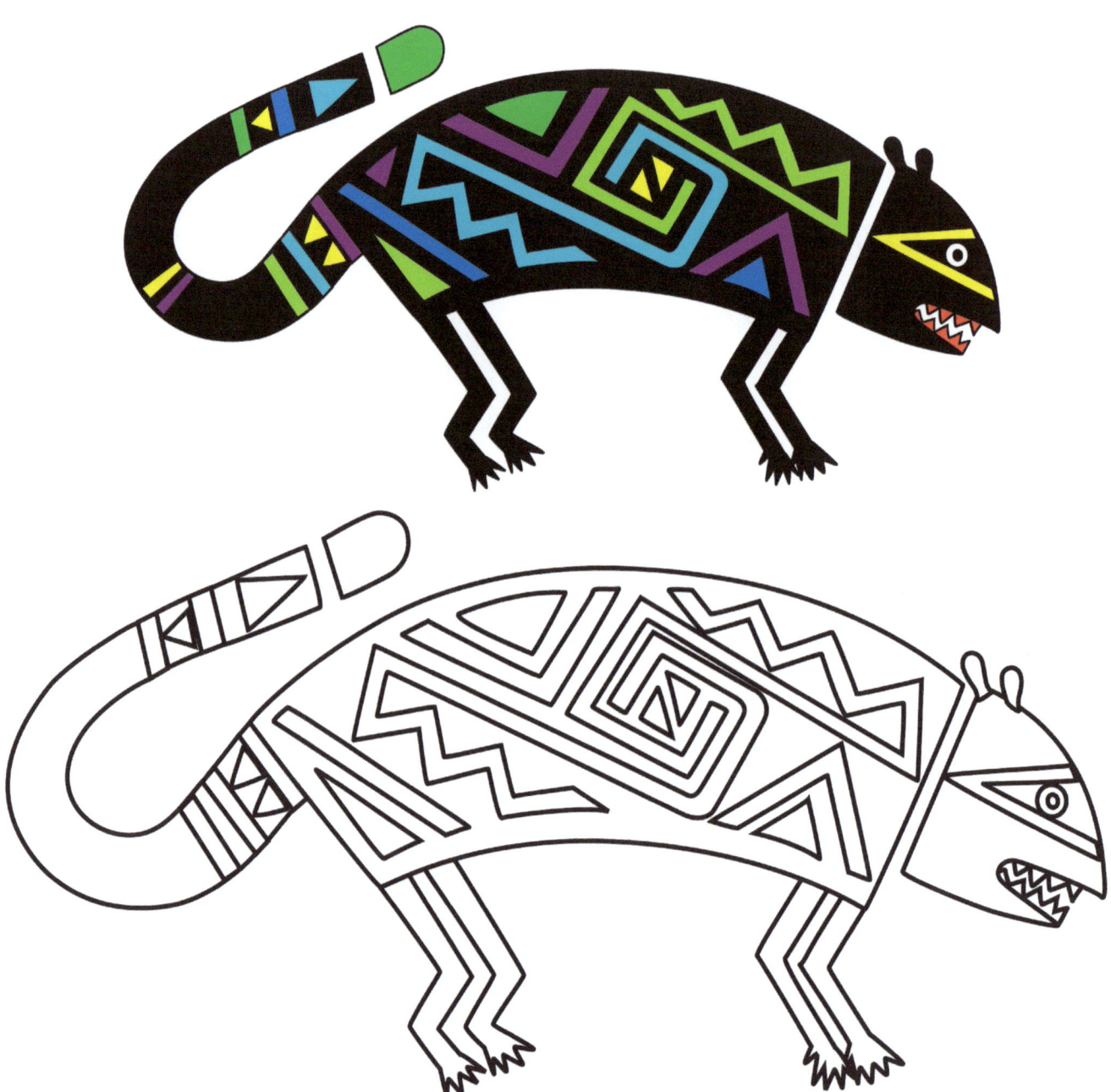

Stylized animal. Pueblo pottery. Southwestern USA.

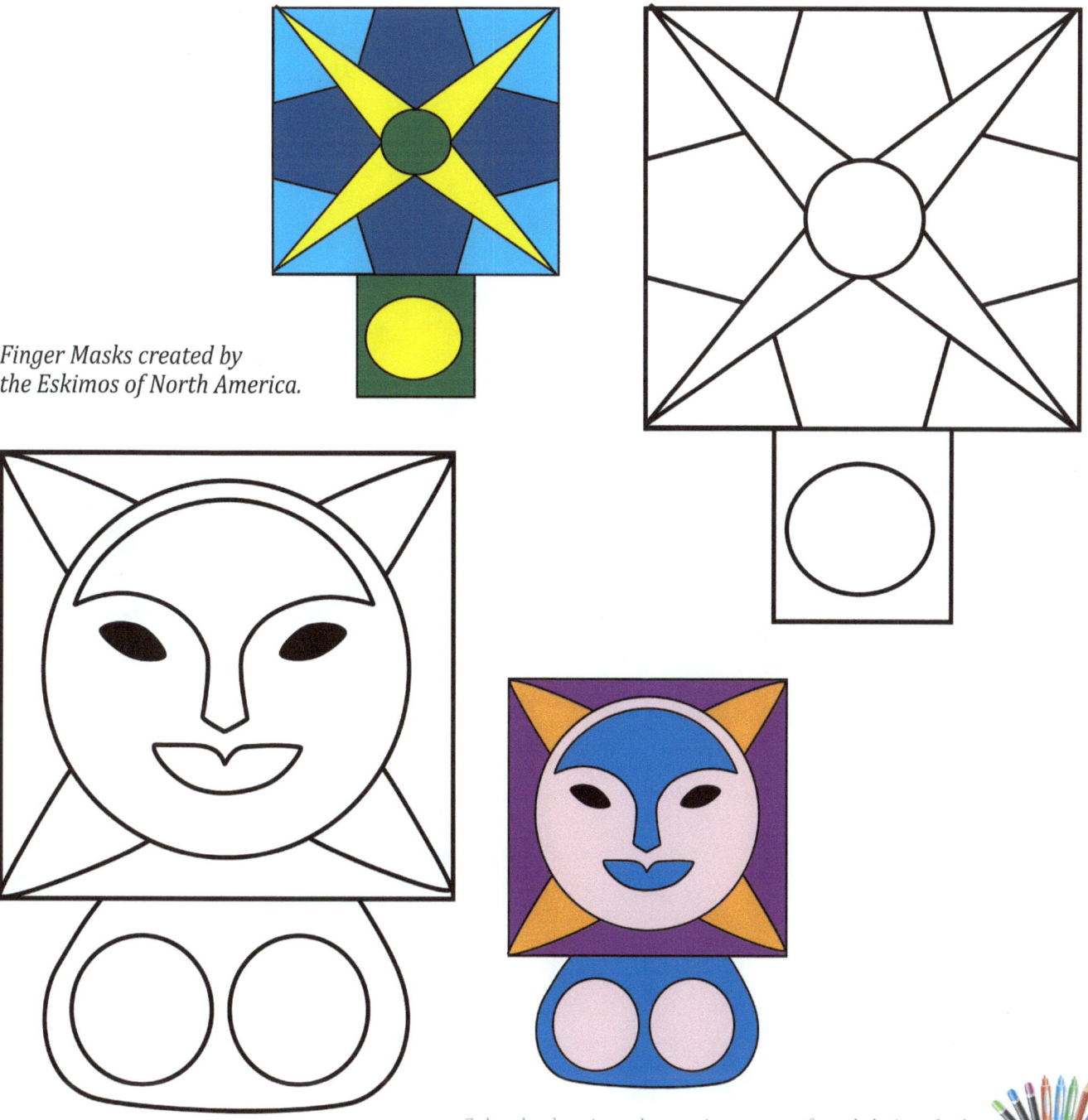

*Finger Masks created by
the Eskimos of North America.*

Color the drawings above using your preferred choice of colors.

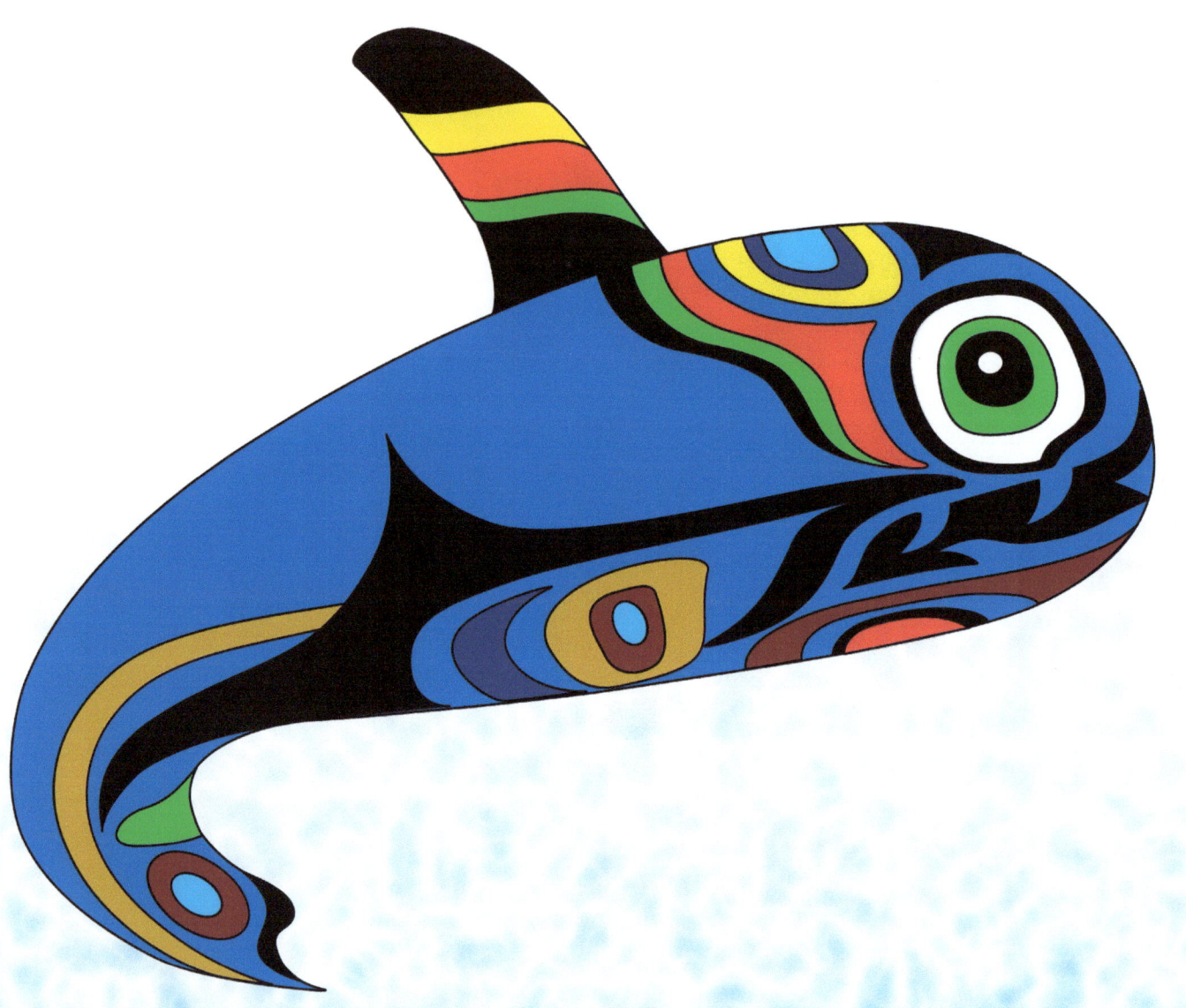

Stylized Killer Whale from a decorated pole. Vancouver Island, Canada.

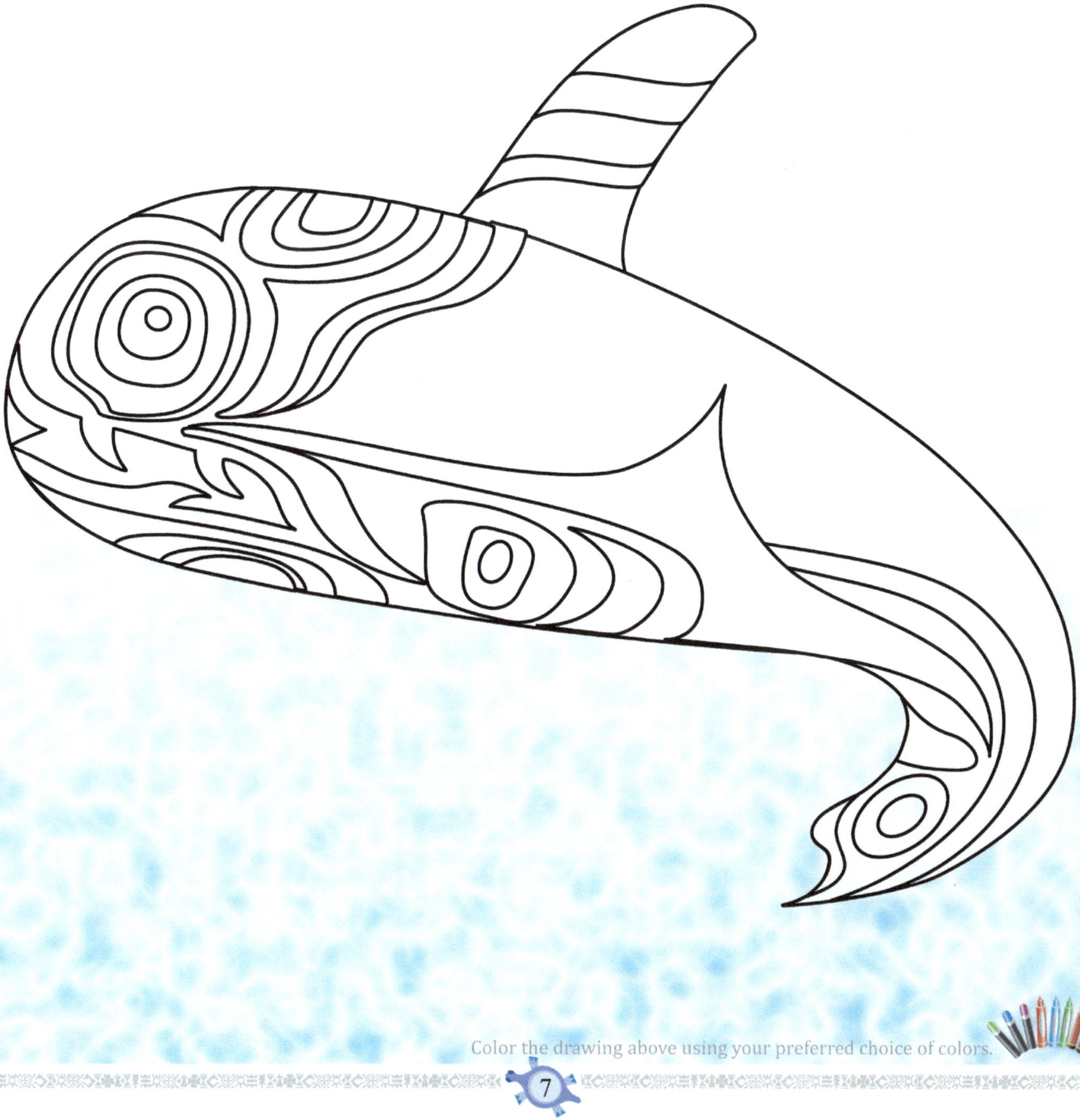

Color the drawing above using your preferred choice of colors.

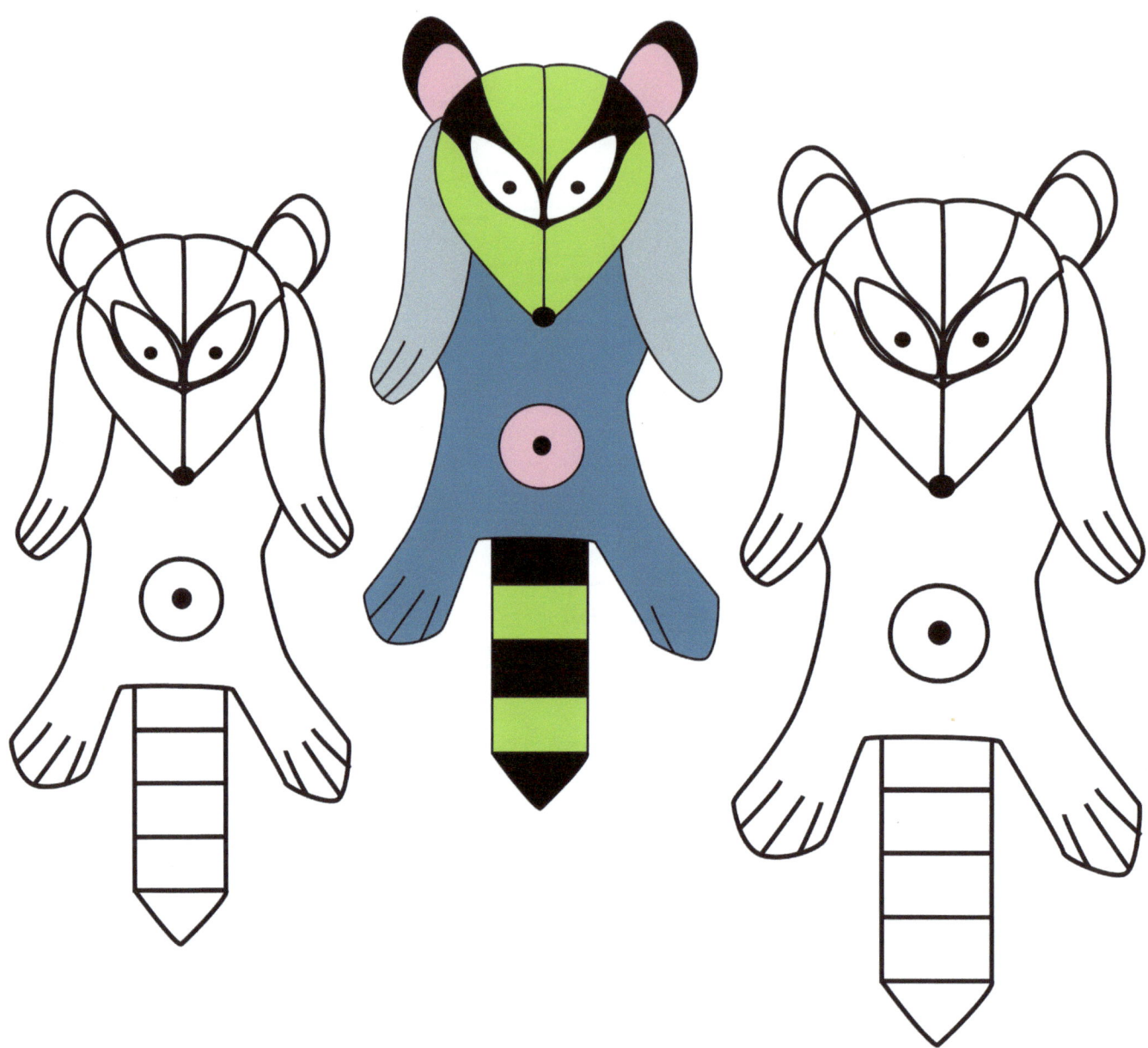

*Facing pages: Image of a raccoon and a
beaver on a button blanket. The beaver is semihuman,
with ears, incisors, and a tail to establish his identity. Northwest Coast.*

American Indian Art

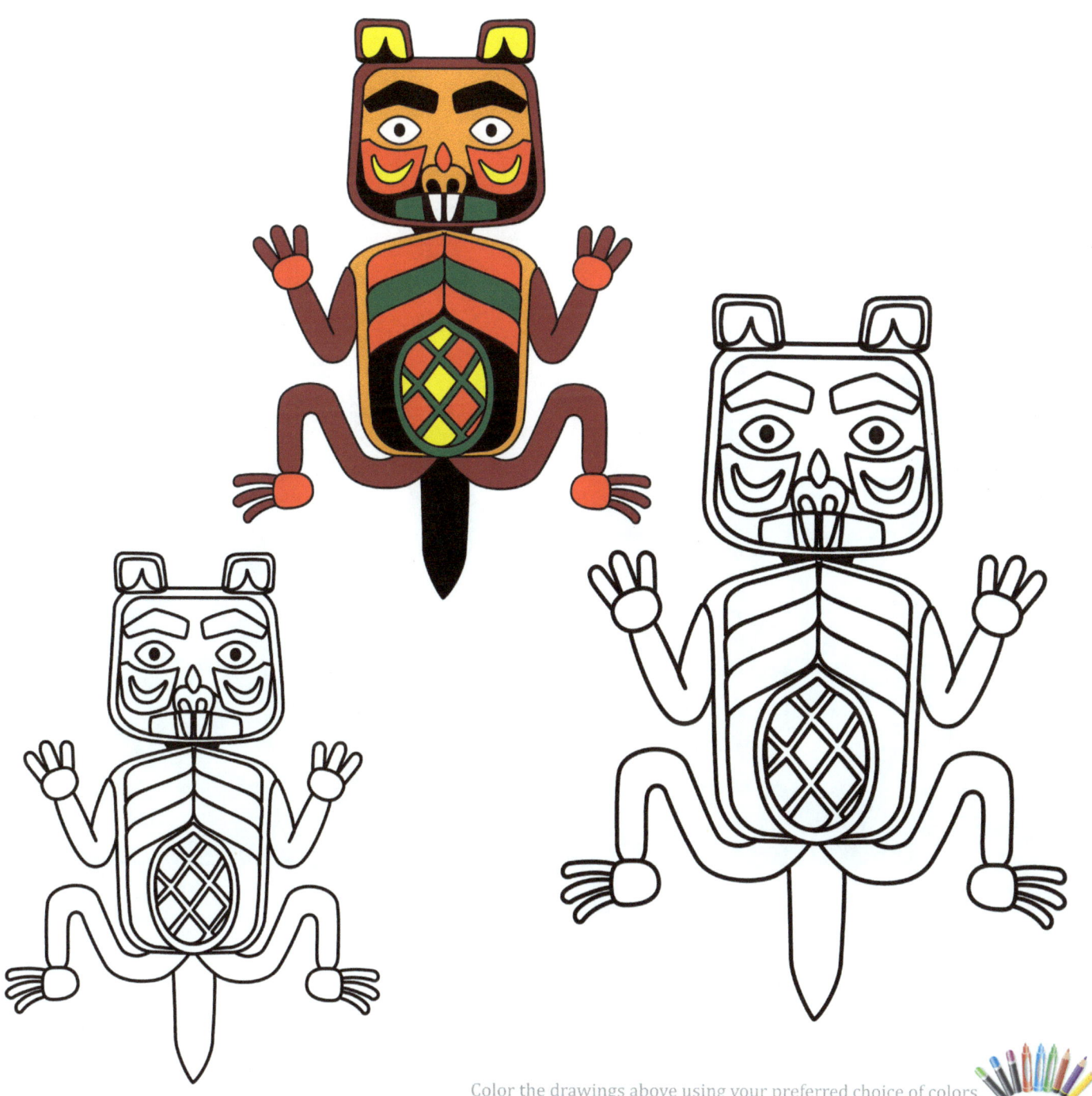

Color the drawings above using your preferred choice of colors.

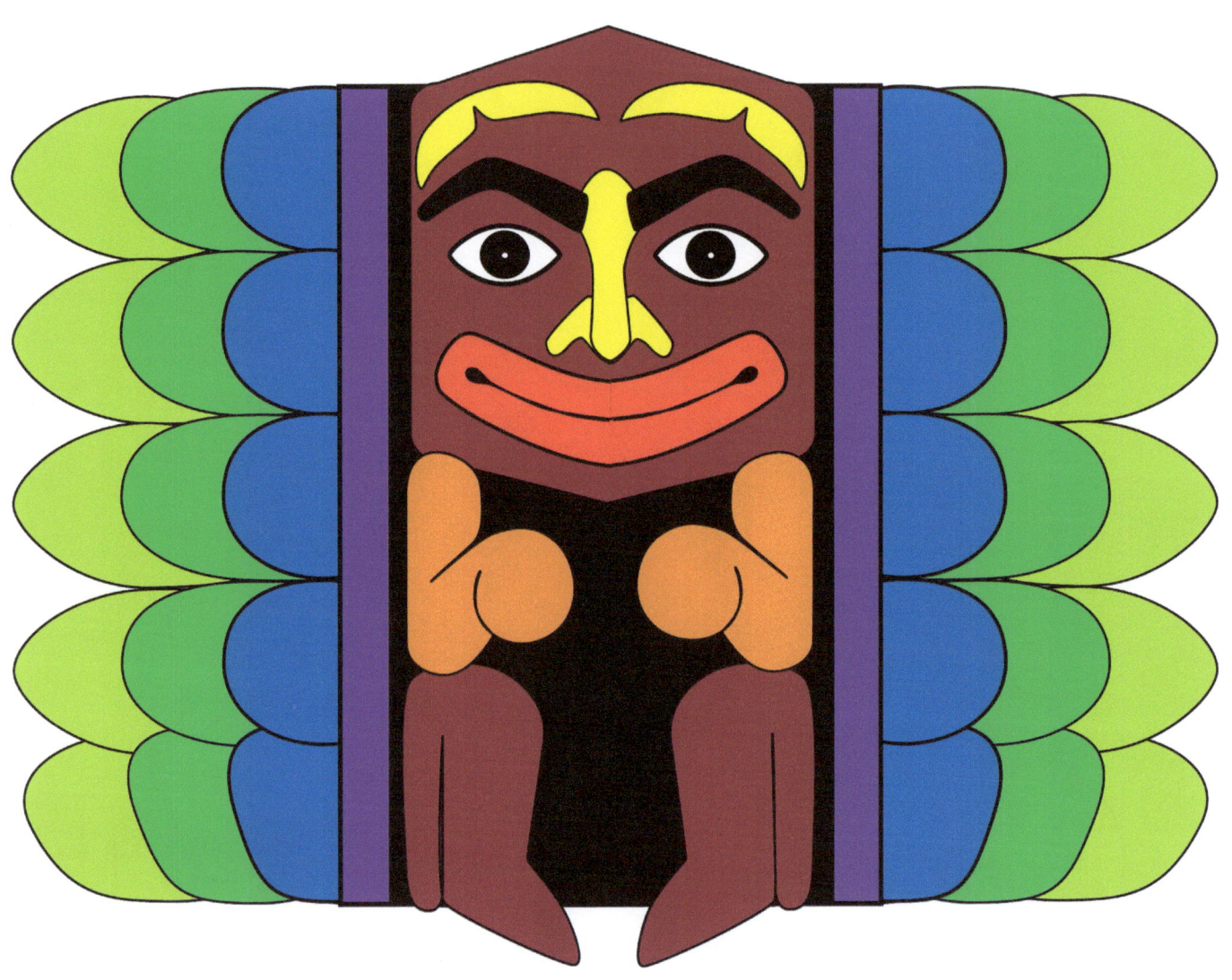

Dance Frontlet, carved and painted on wood
representing a bear. Tlingit Tribe, Northwest Coast. Late 19th Century.

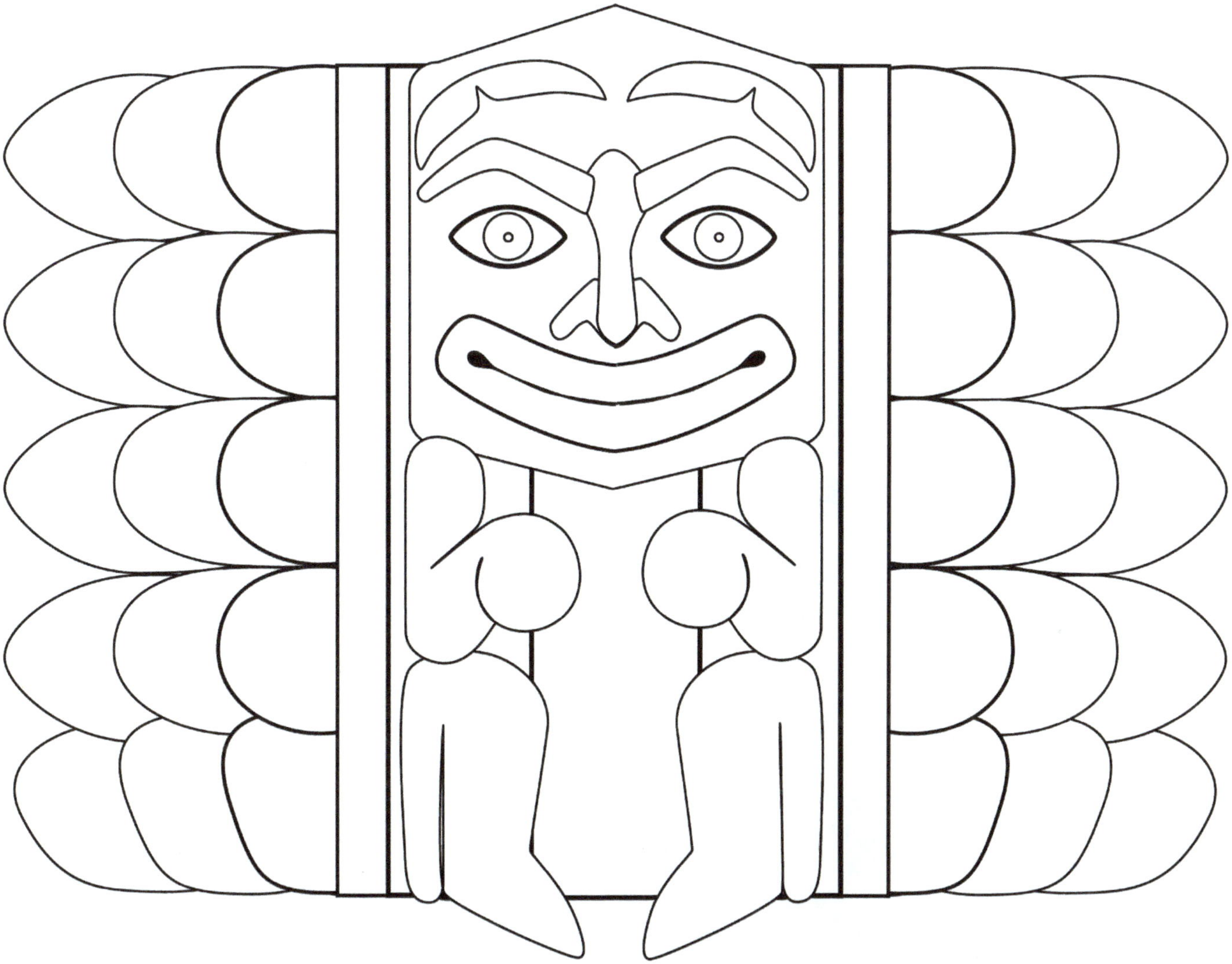

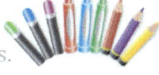

Color the drawing above using your preferred choice of colors.

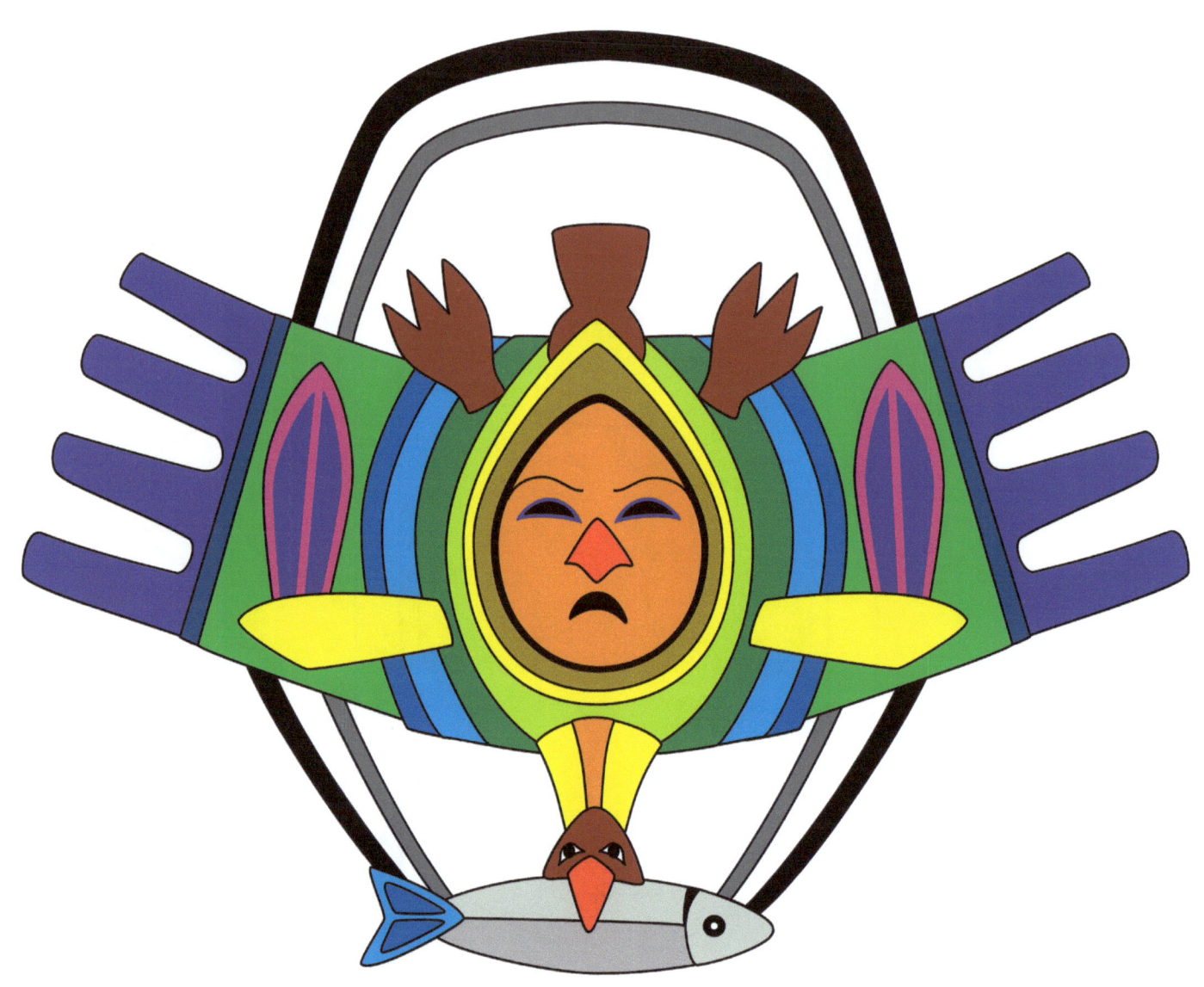

Eskimos in Goodnews Bay and in Hooper Bay (Alaska),
used to wear this mask. It represents a falcon holding a fish.

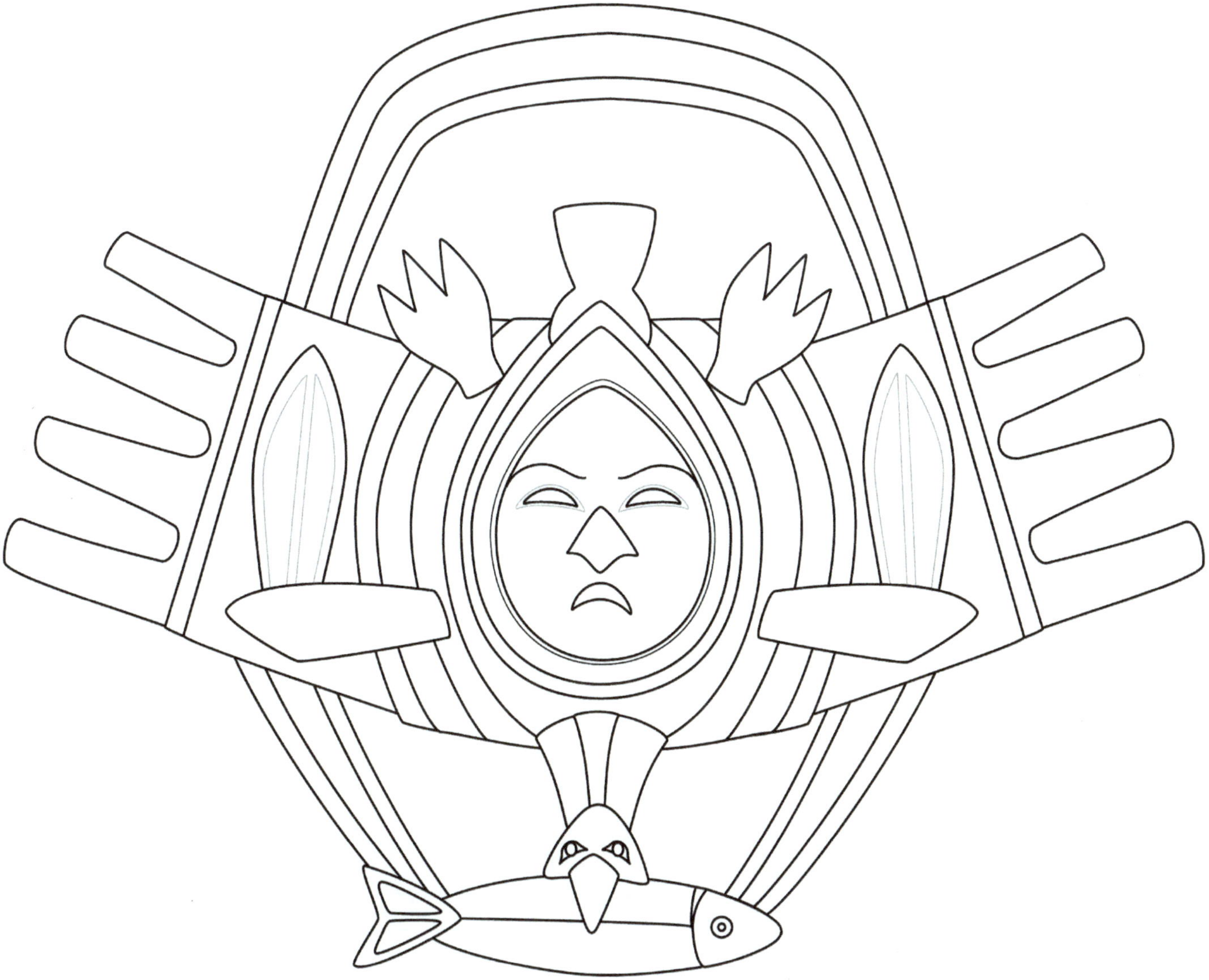

Color the drawing above using your preferred choice of colors.

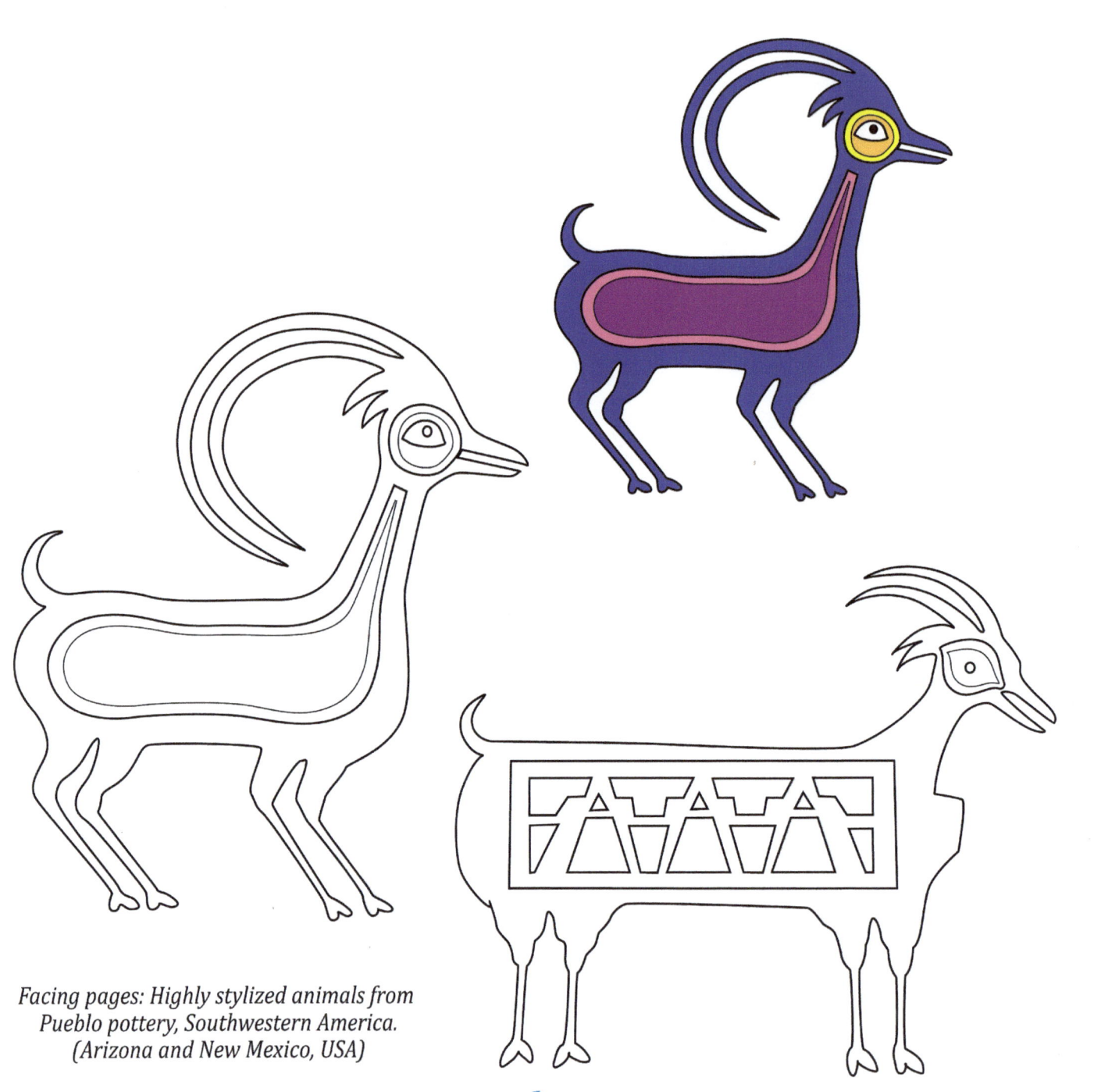

Facing pages: Highly stylized animals from Pueblo pottery, Southwestern America. (Arizona and New Mexico, USA)

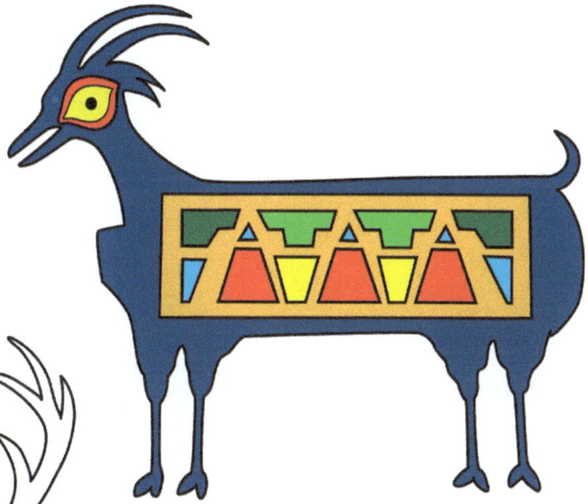

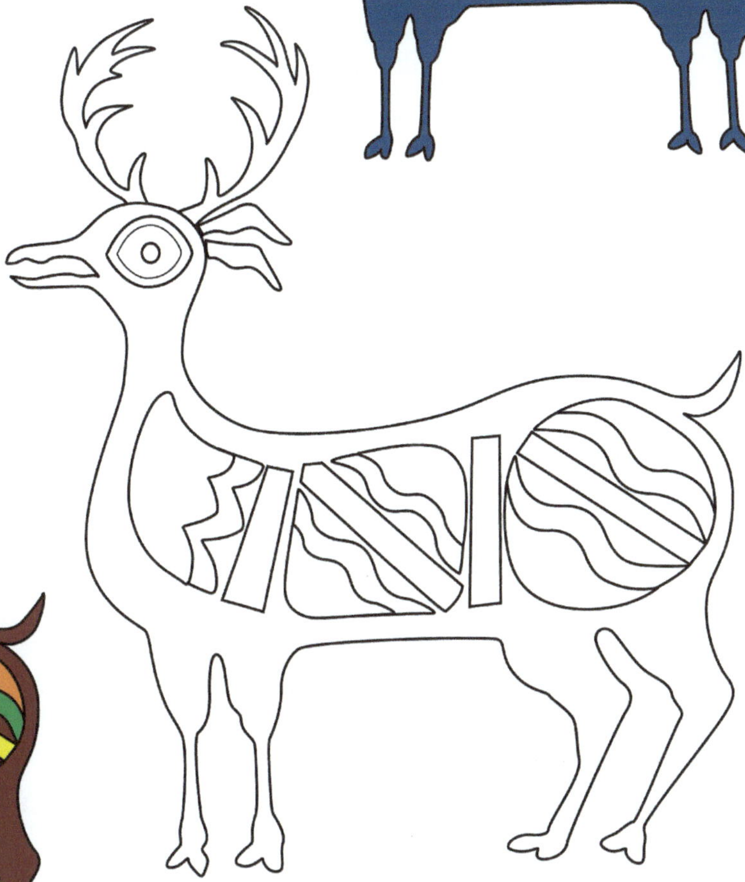

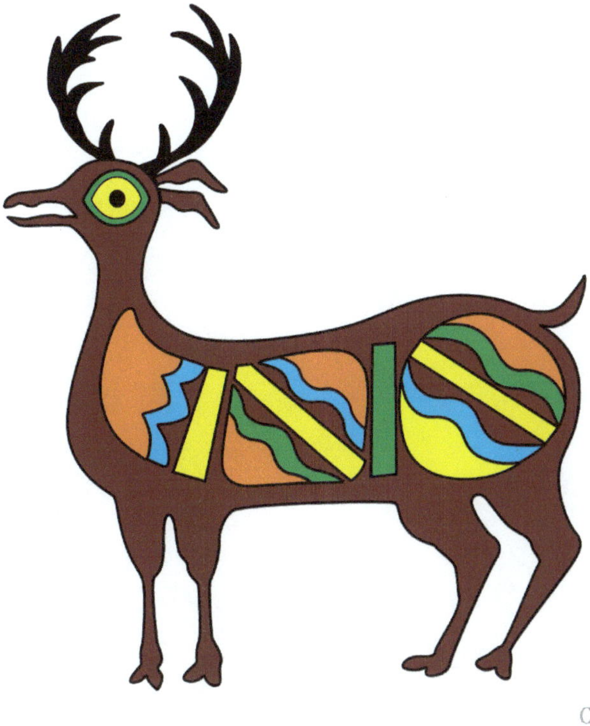

Color the drawings above using your preferred choice of colors.

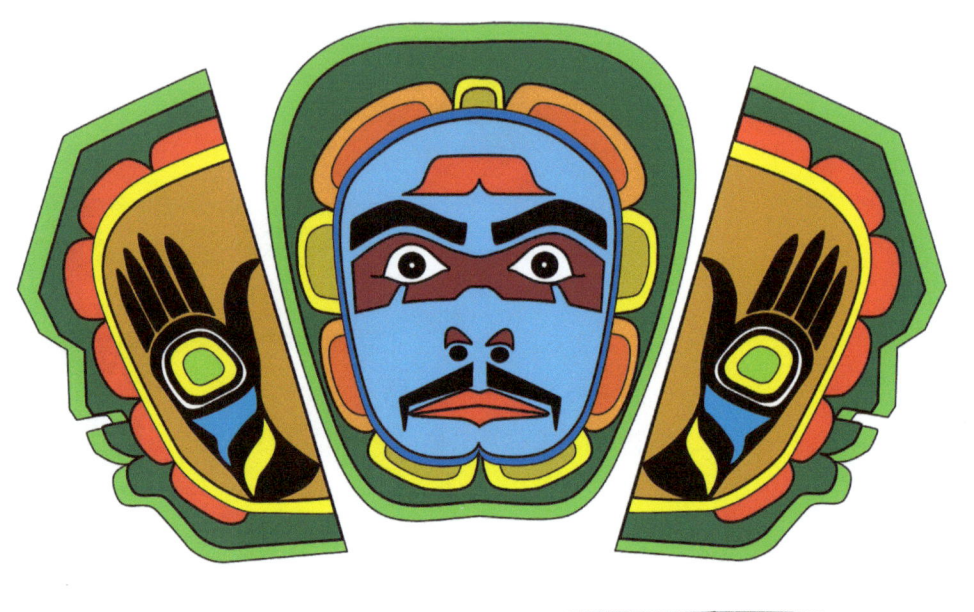

Kwakiutl transformation mask, associated with the Born-to-be-Head-of-the-World. Vancouver Island, Canada.

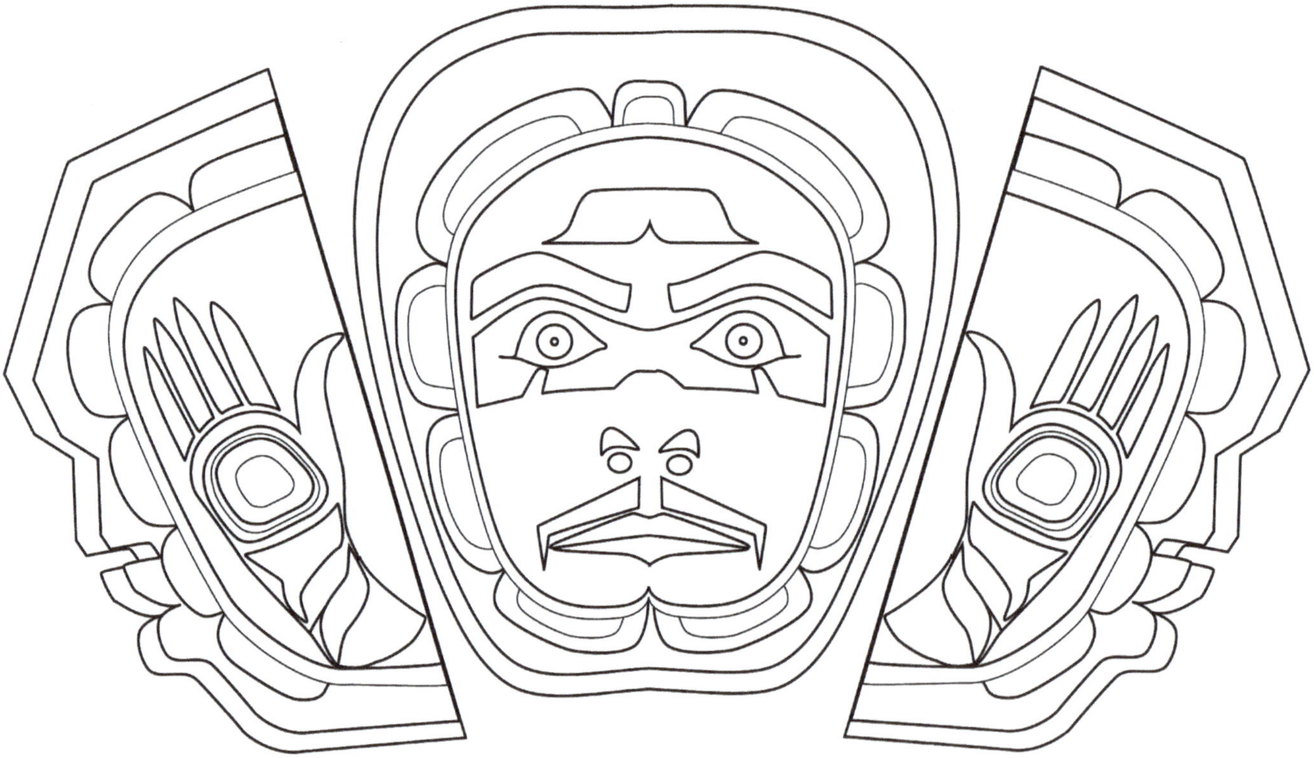

The famed Hopi potter Nampeyo adopted prehistoric motifs in the 20th Century. The image is abstracted body parts and feathers of a bird, Southwest USA.

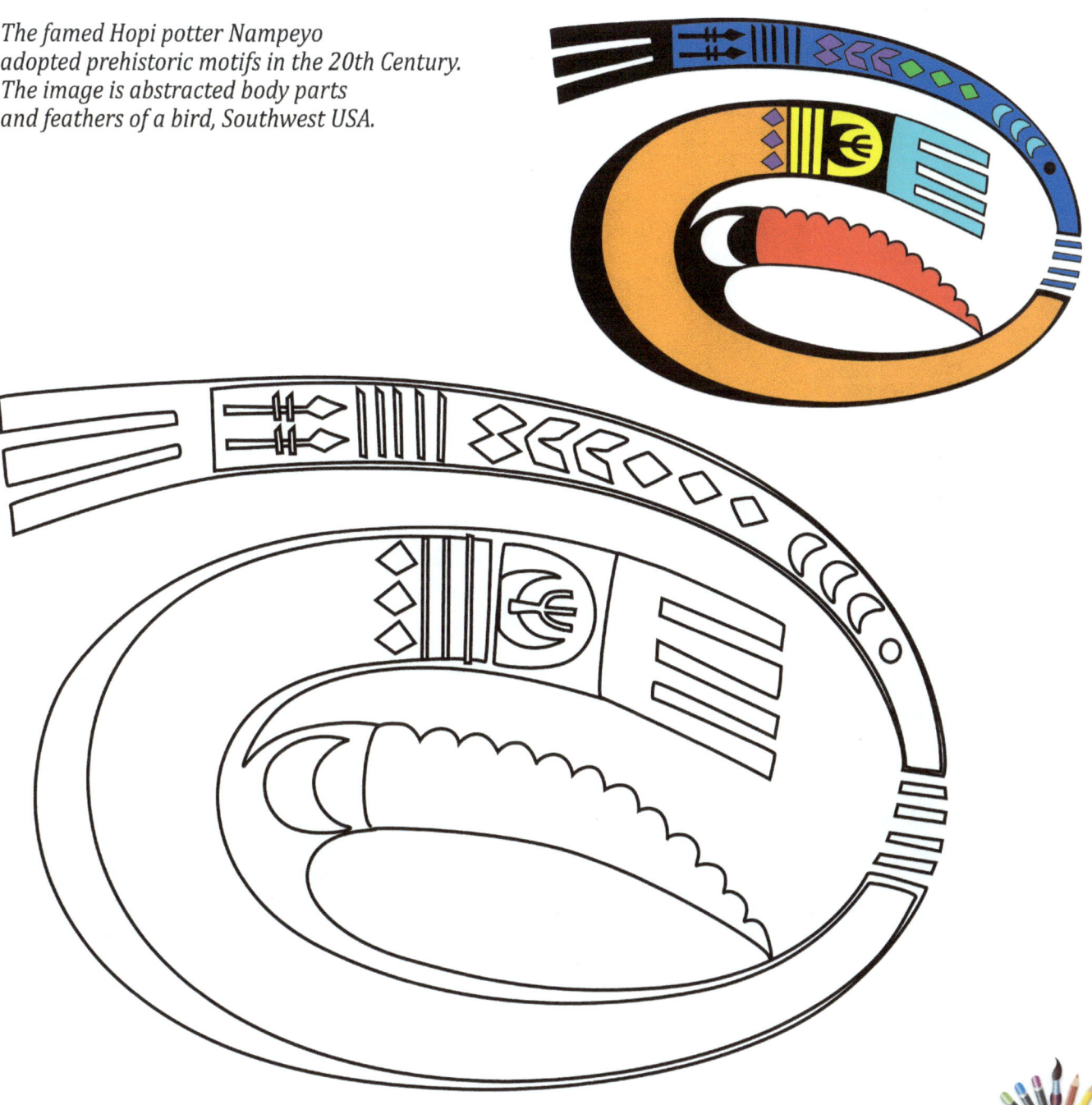

Color the drawings above using your preferred choice of colors.

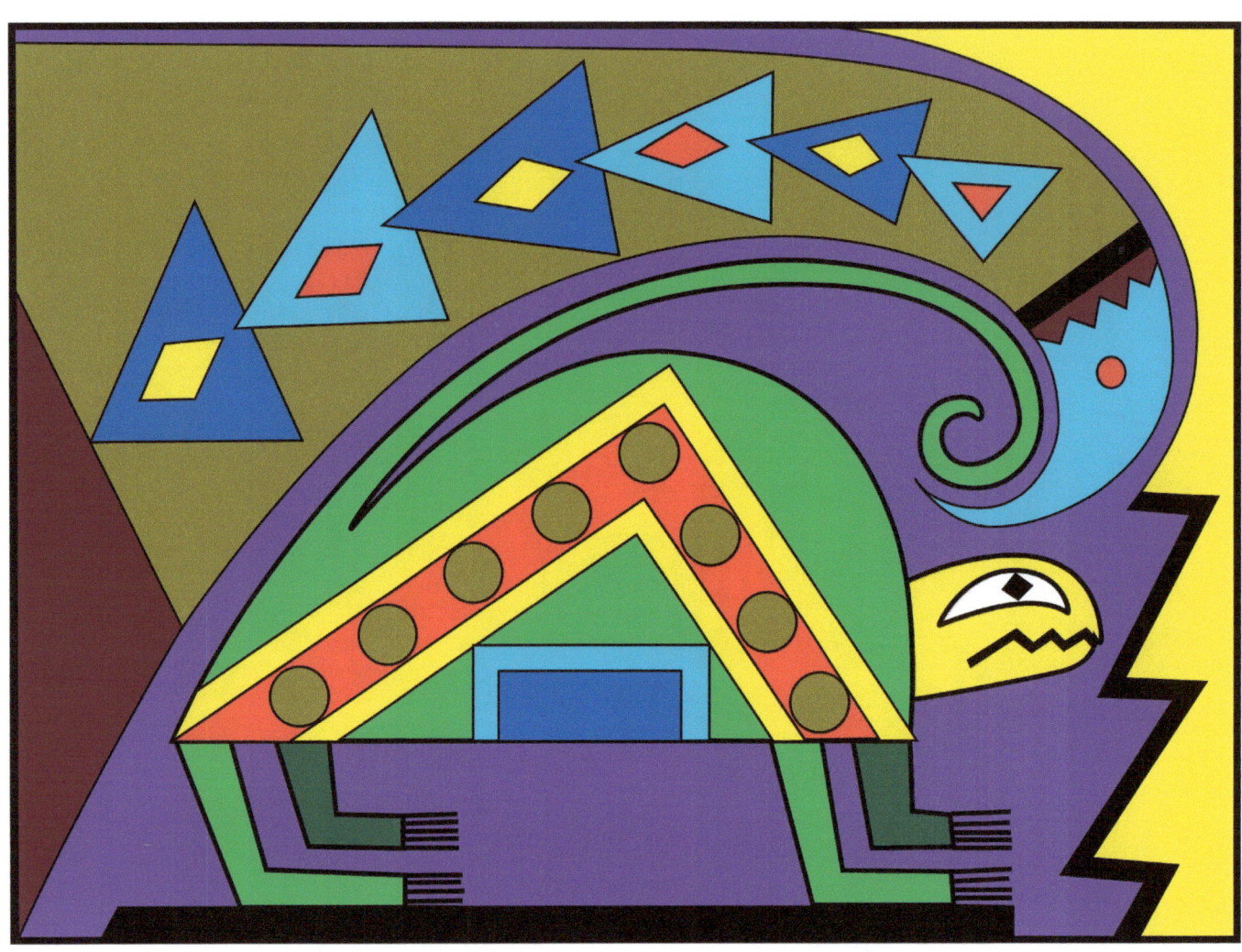

From an American Native painting. The painter explores ancient beliefs and anthropomorphized forces of nature as depicted in Hopi, Navajo, and ancient Mimbres cultures.

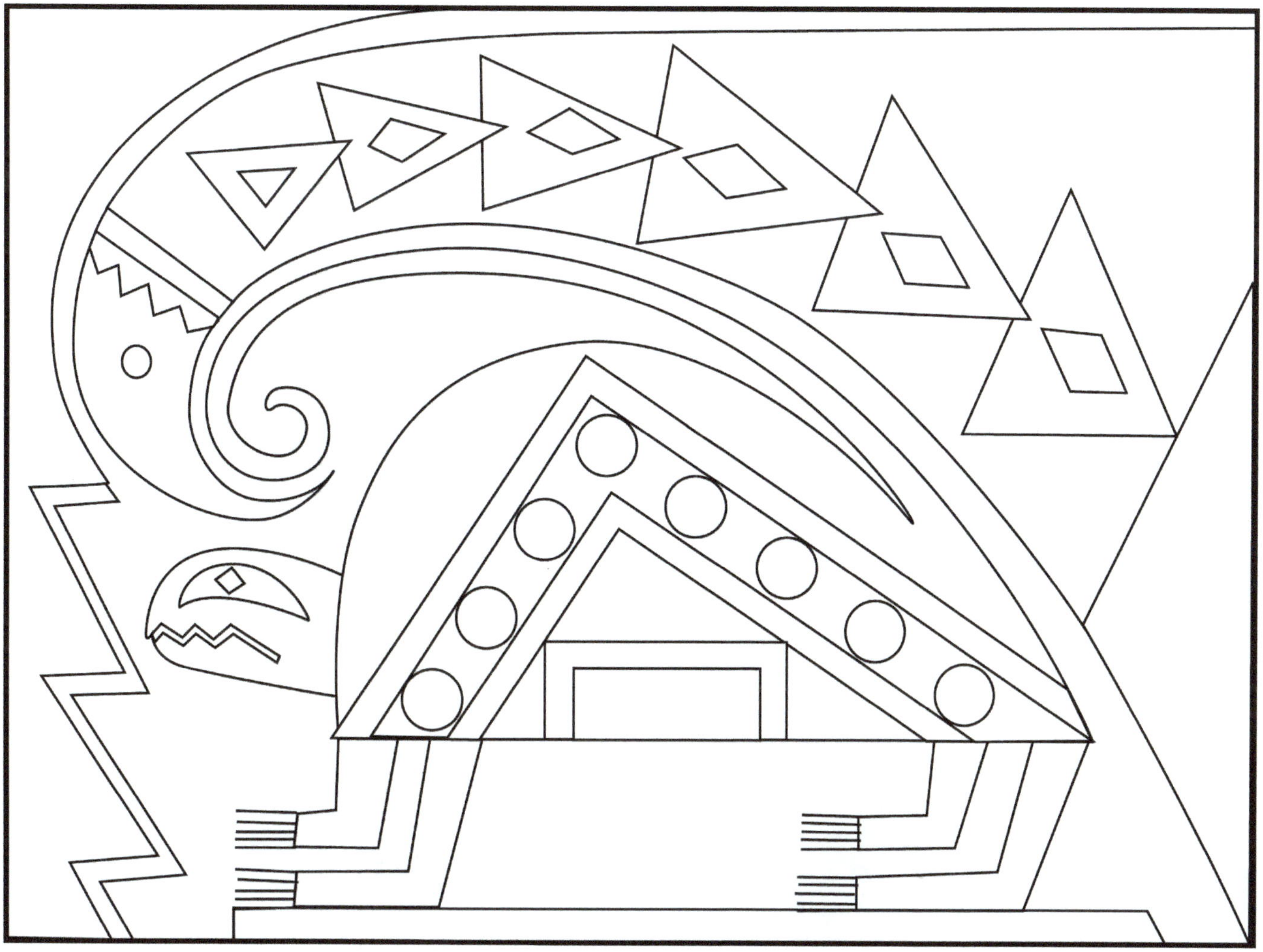

Color the drawing above using your preferred choice of colors.

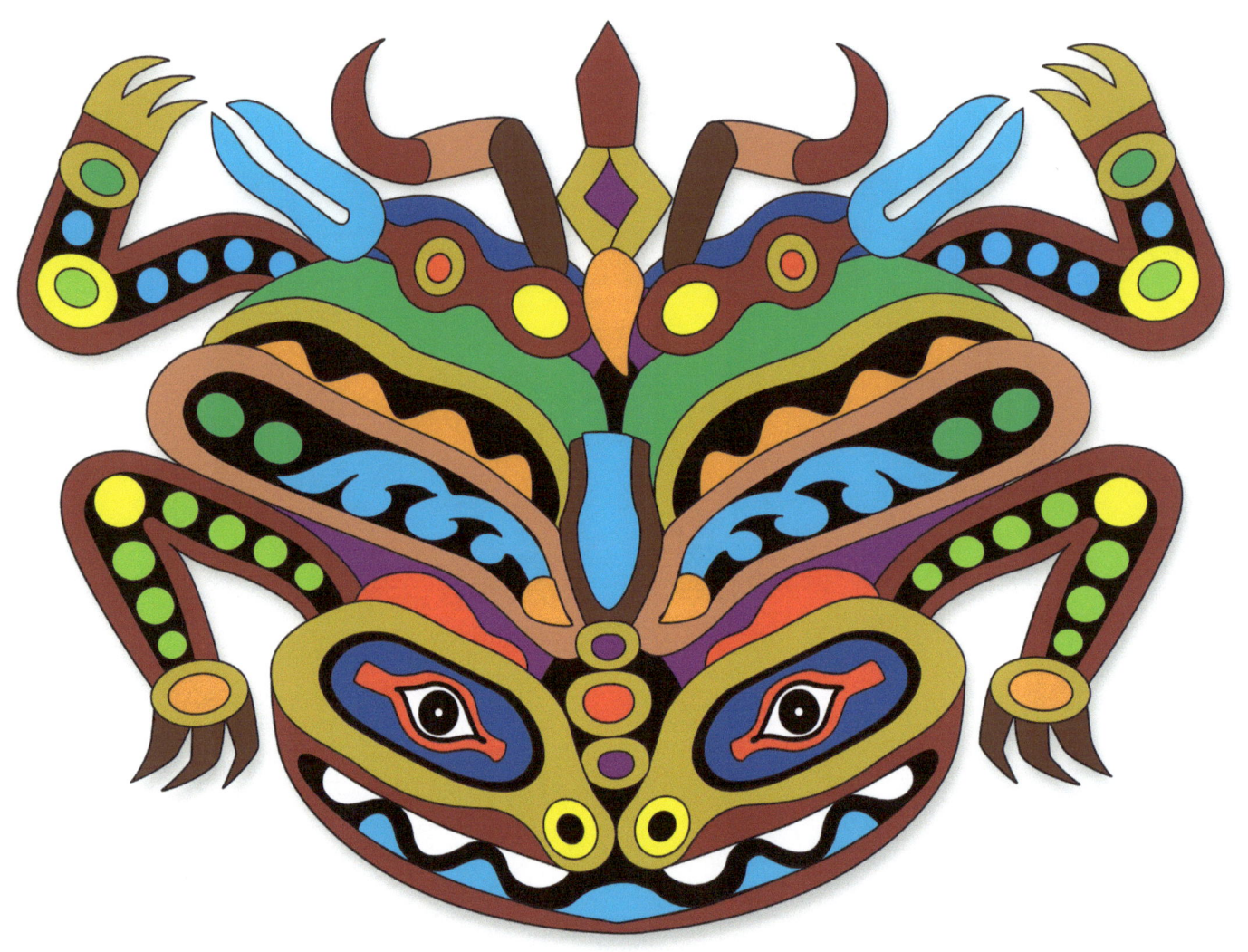

Frog on leggings, illustrating the flamboyant quality of the style. Tlingit, 1880 C.E.

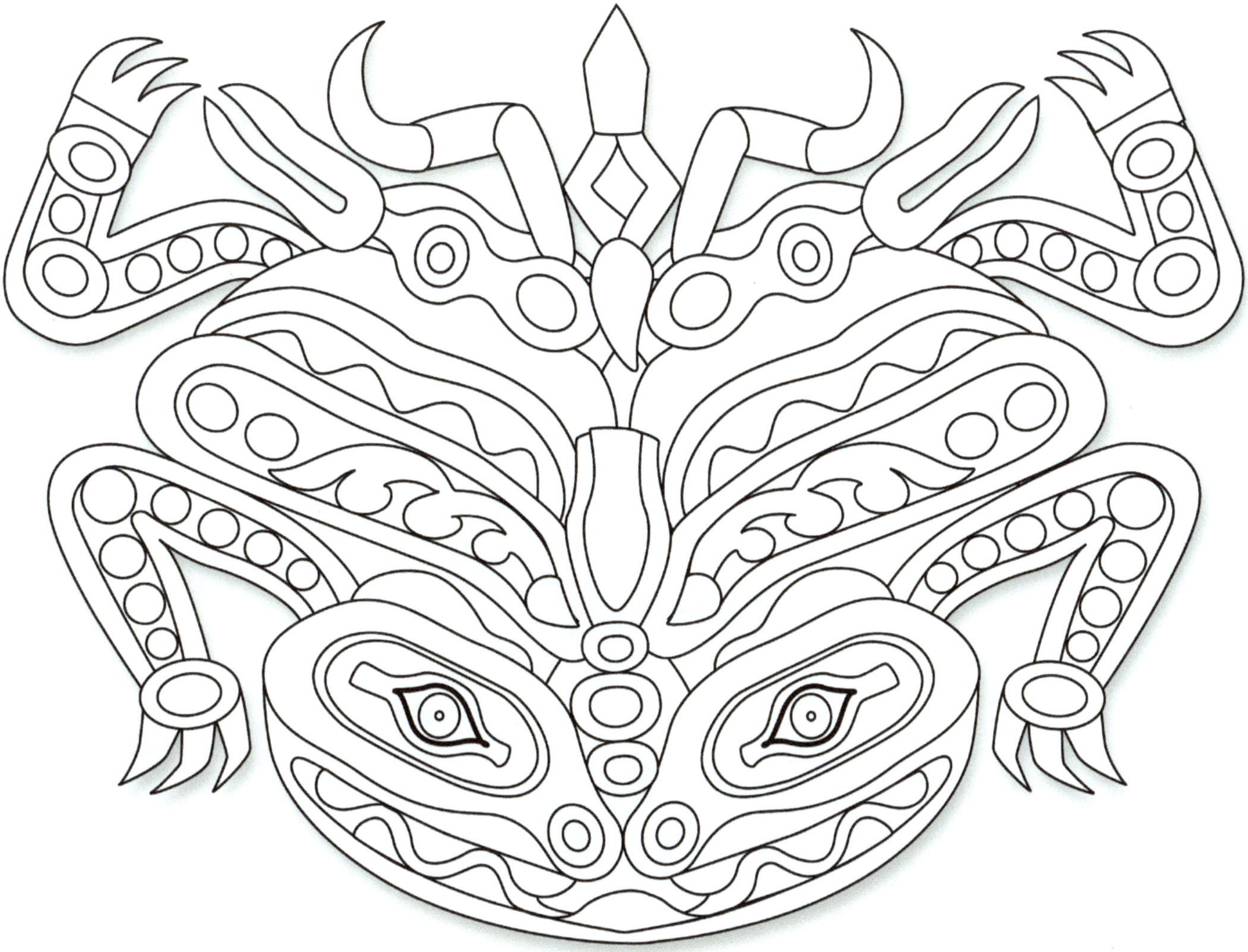

Color the drawing above using your preferred choice of colors.

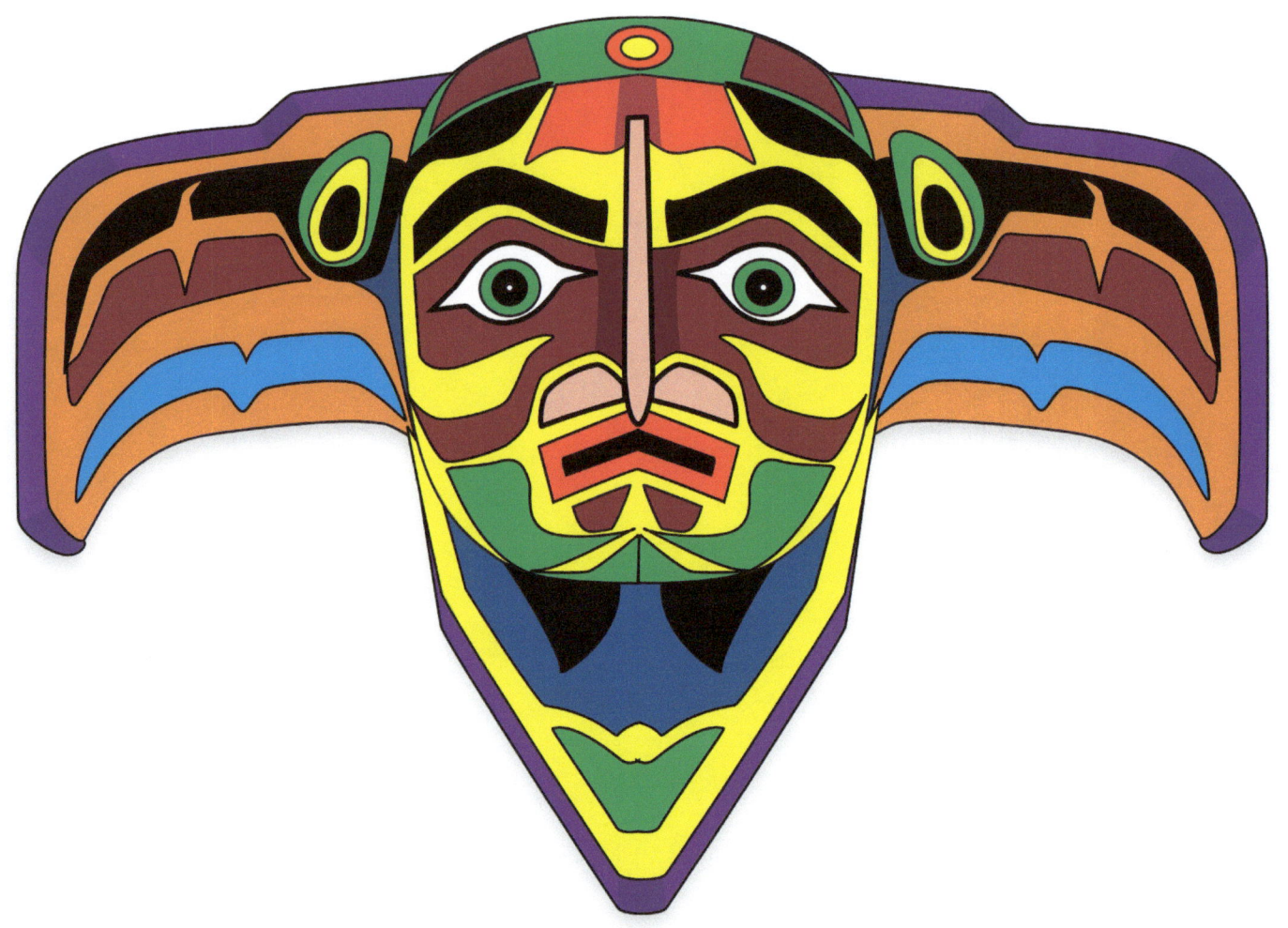

One of the most dramatic types of art displayed
at a potlatch was this transformation mask.
It represents a legend from its owner's family history.
When shut, it depicts an eagle, when open, it reveals
a humanoid face. Vancouver Island, Canada.

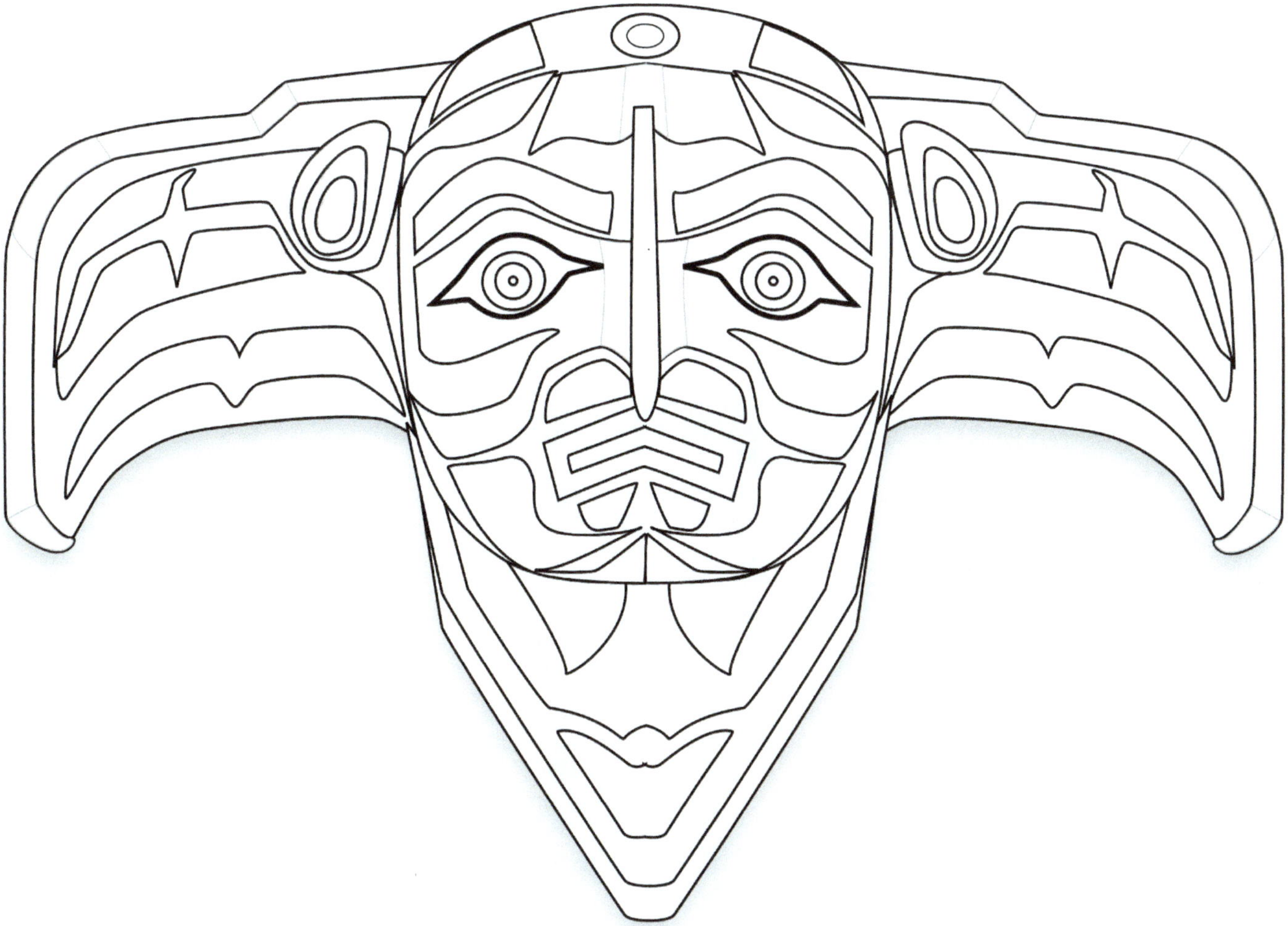

Color the drawing above using your preferred choice of colors.

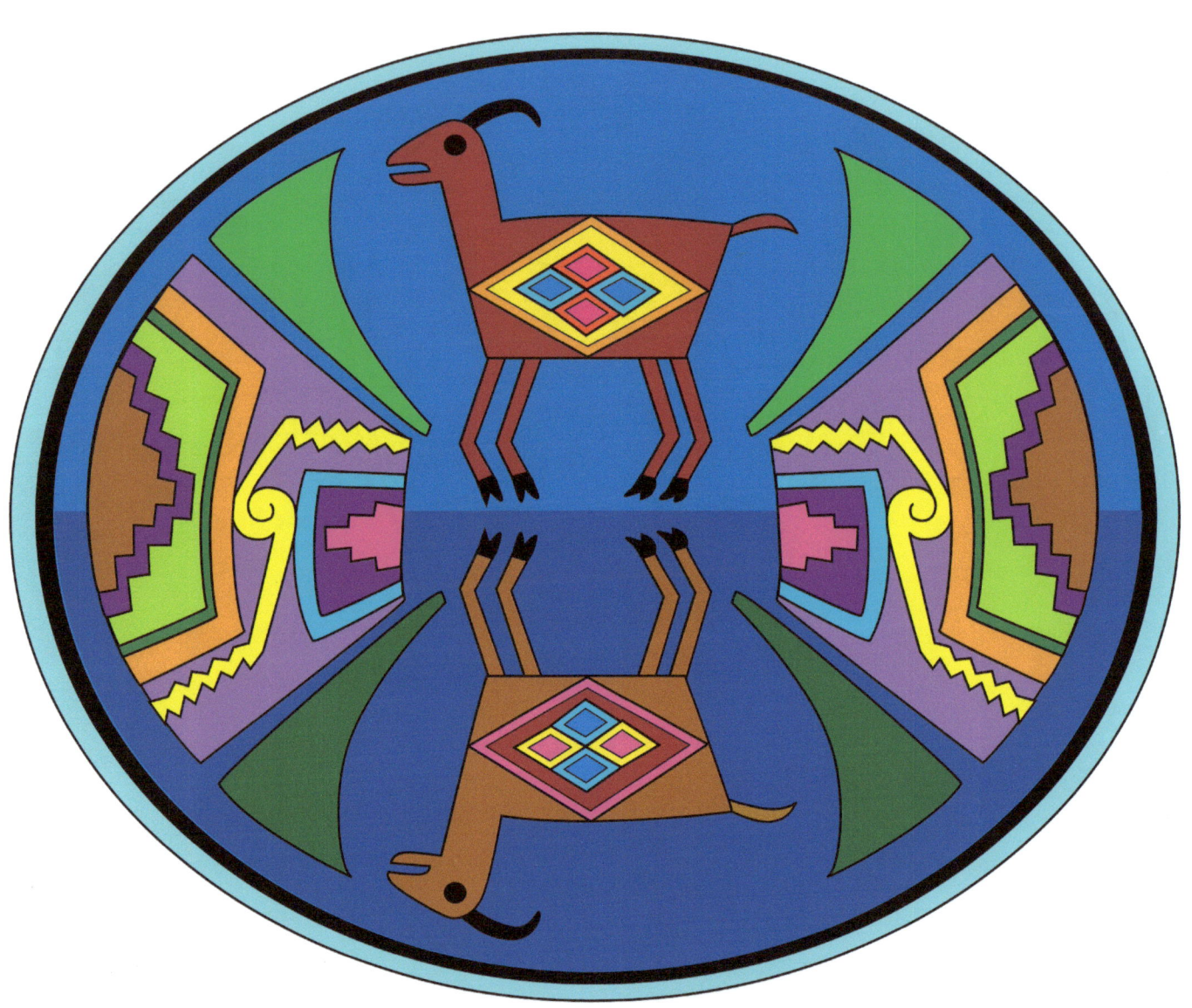

Highly stylized drawing of Mountain Goat and
other elements on a bowl by Mimbres potter. New Mexico, USA.
Southwestern pottery paintings existed even before 1200 B.C.E.

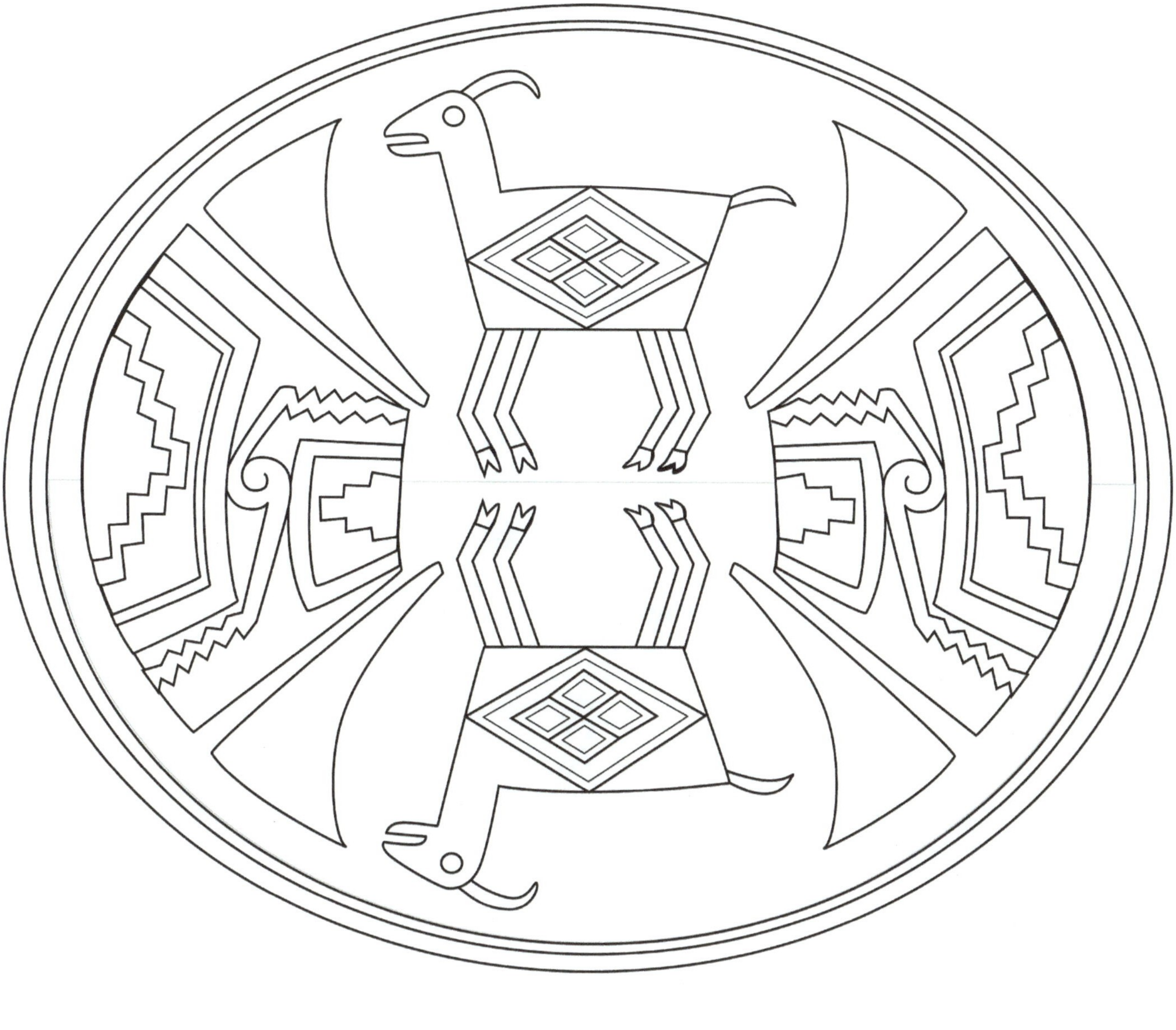

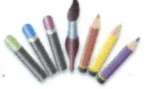

Color the drawing above using your preferred choice of colors.

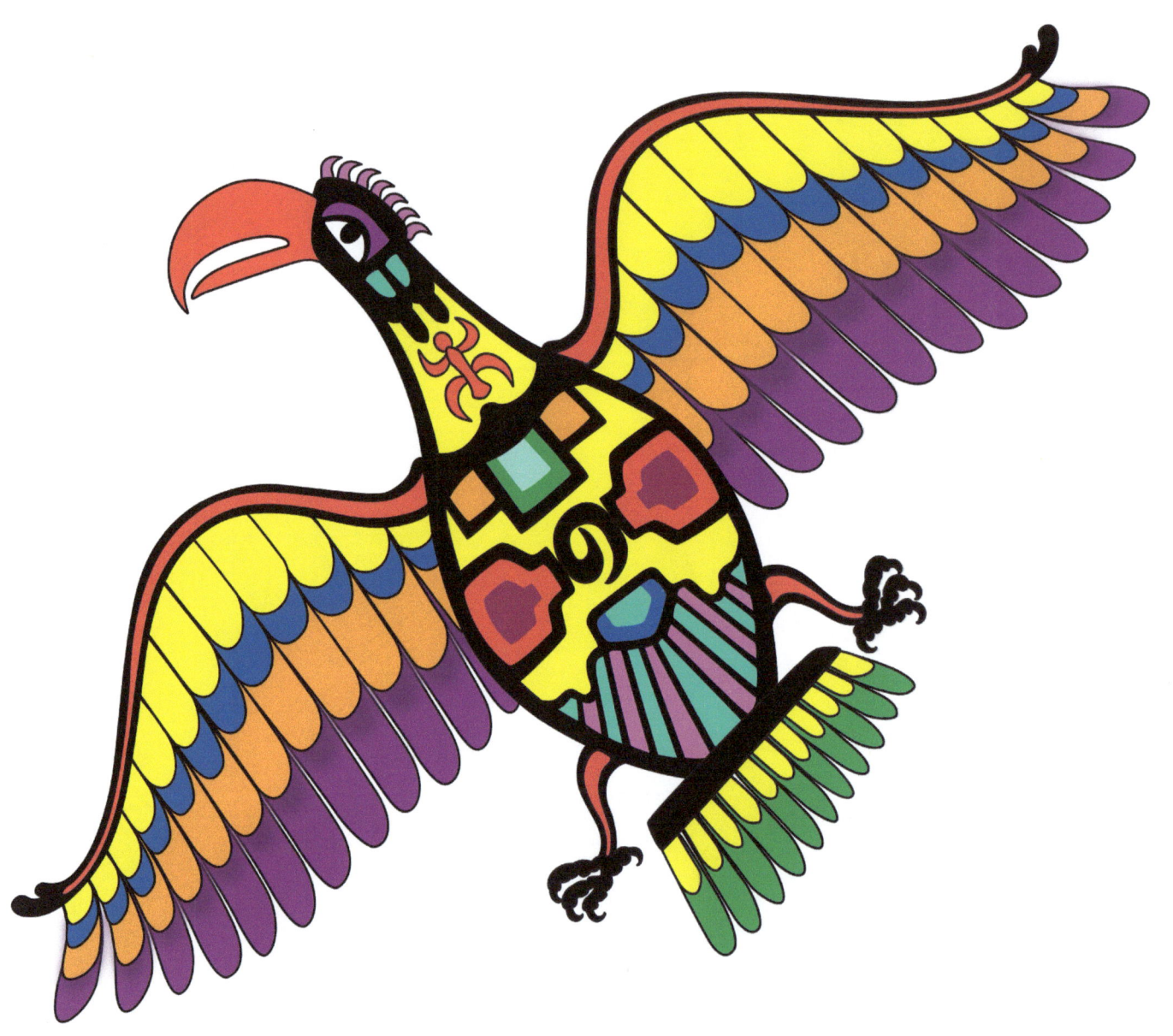

*Image of a Thunderbird on a house screen, displayed
at potlatches and other significant occasions. Western Canada, 1850 C.E.*

American Indian Art

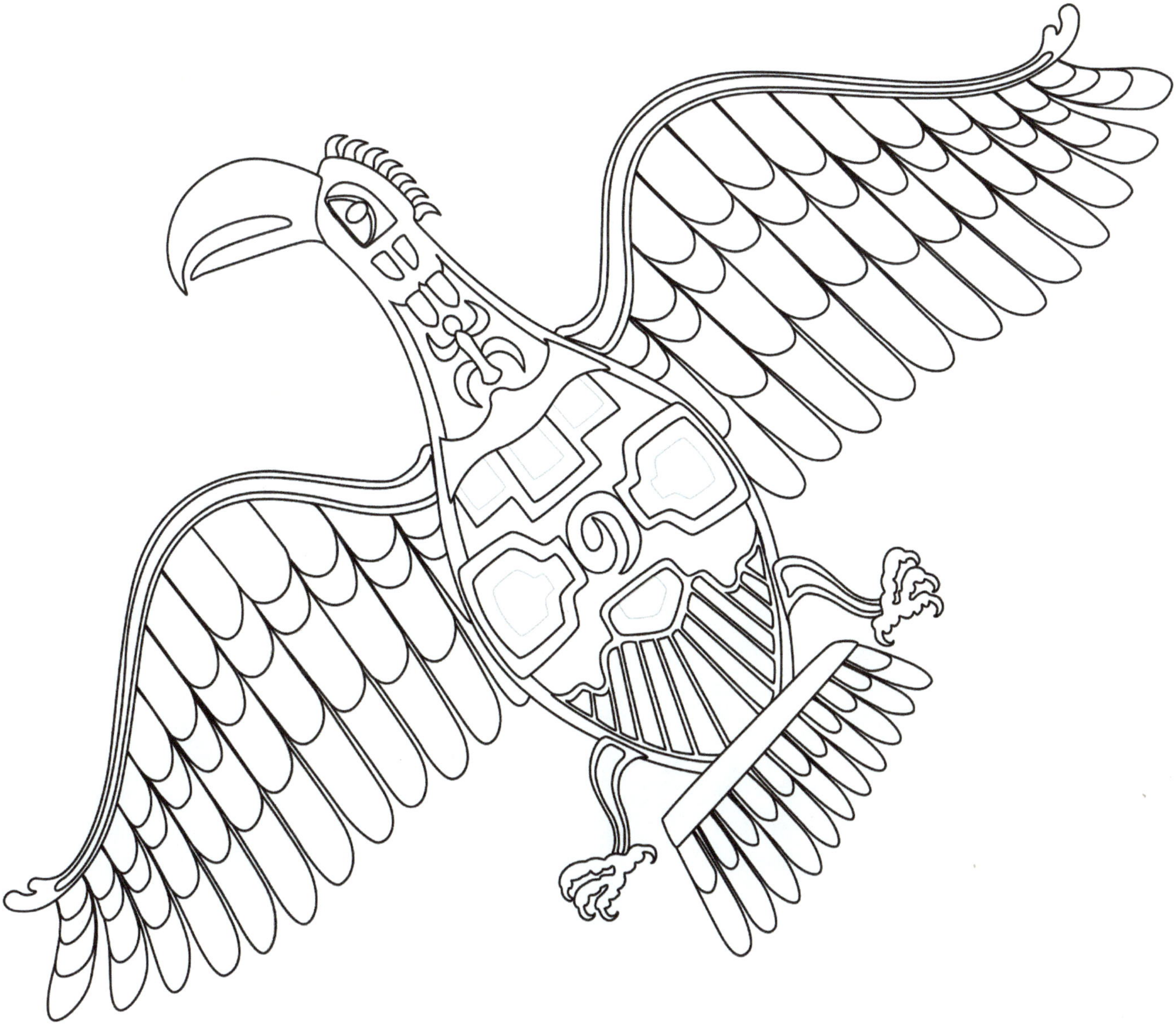

Color the drawing above using your preferred choice of colors.

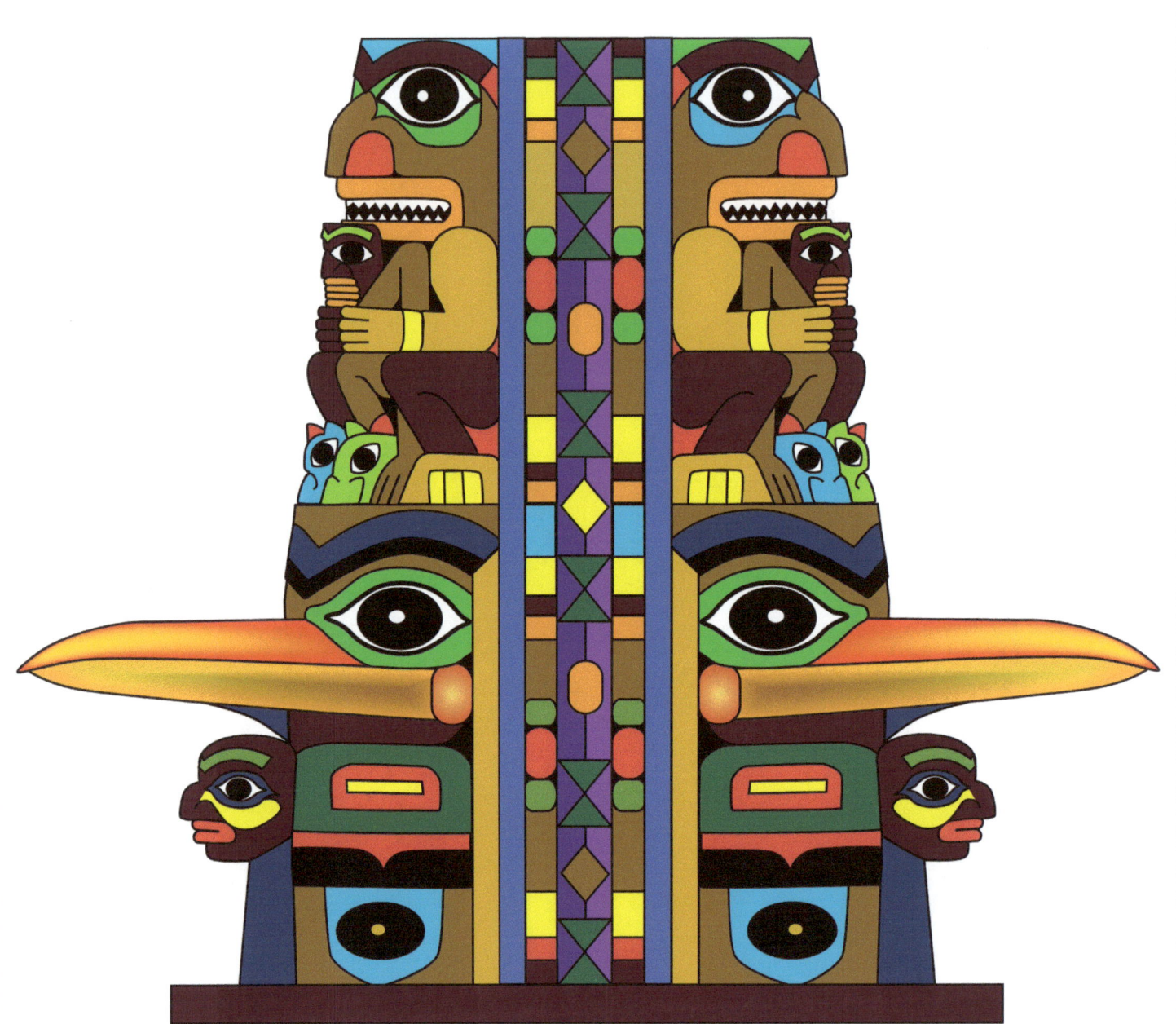

Part of a Haida Heraldic or Totem Pole. When a person of dignitary dies, his successor or other family members raise a pole in his honor. Vancouver Island, Canada.

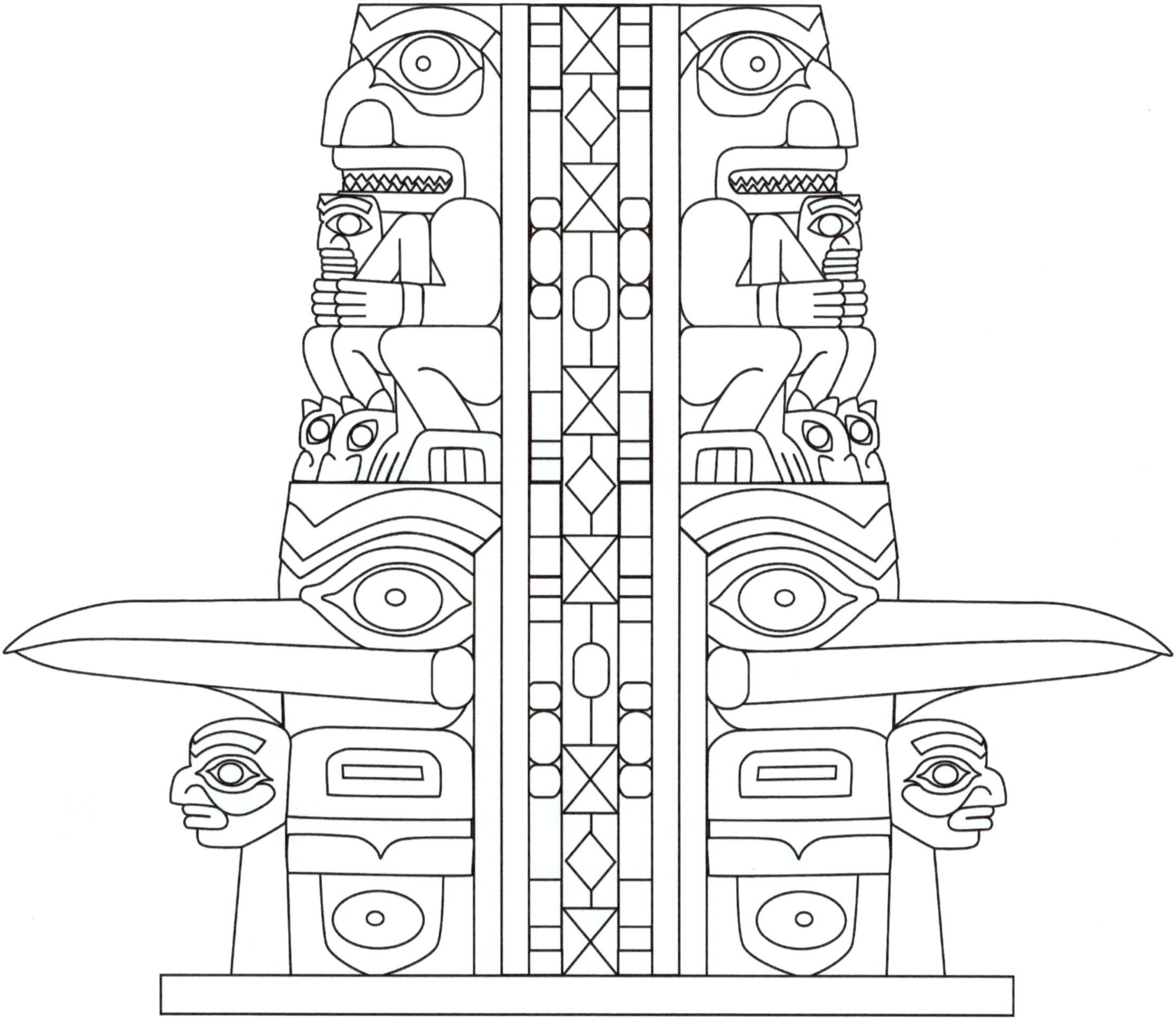

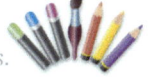

Color the drawing above using your preferred choice of colors.

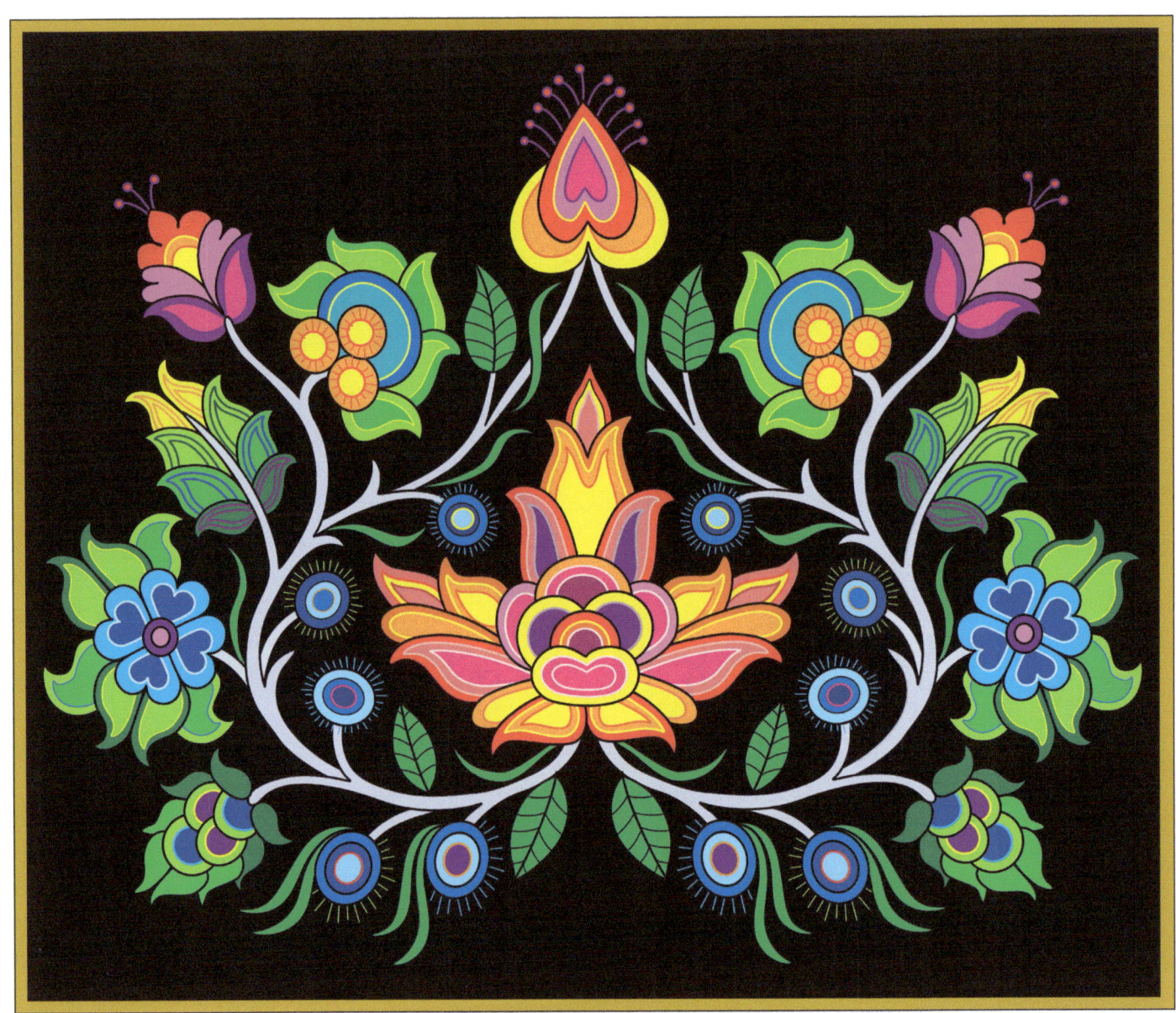

Floral designs on men's leggings. Floral motifs replaced
earlier geometric and spirit designs in Woodlands art during 19th Century C.E.

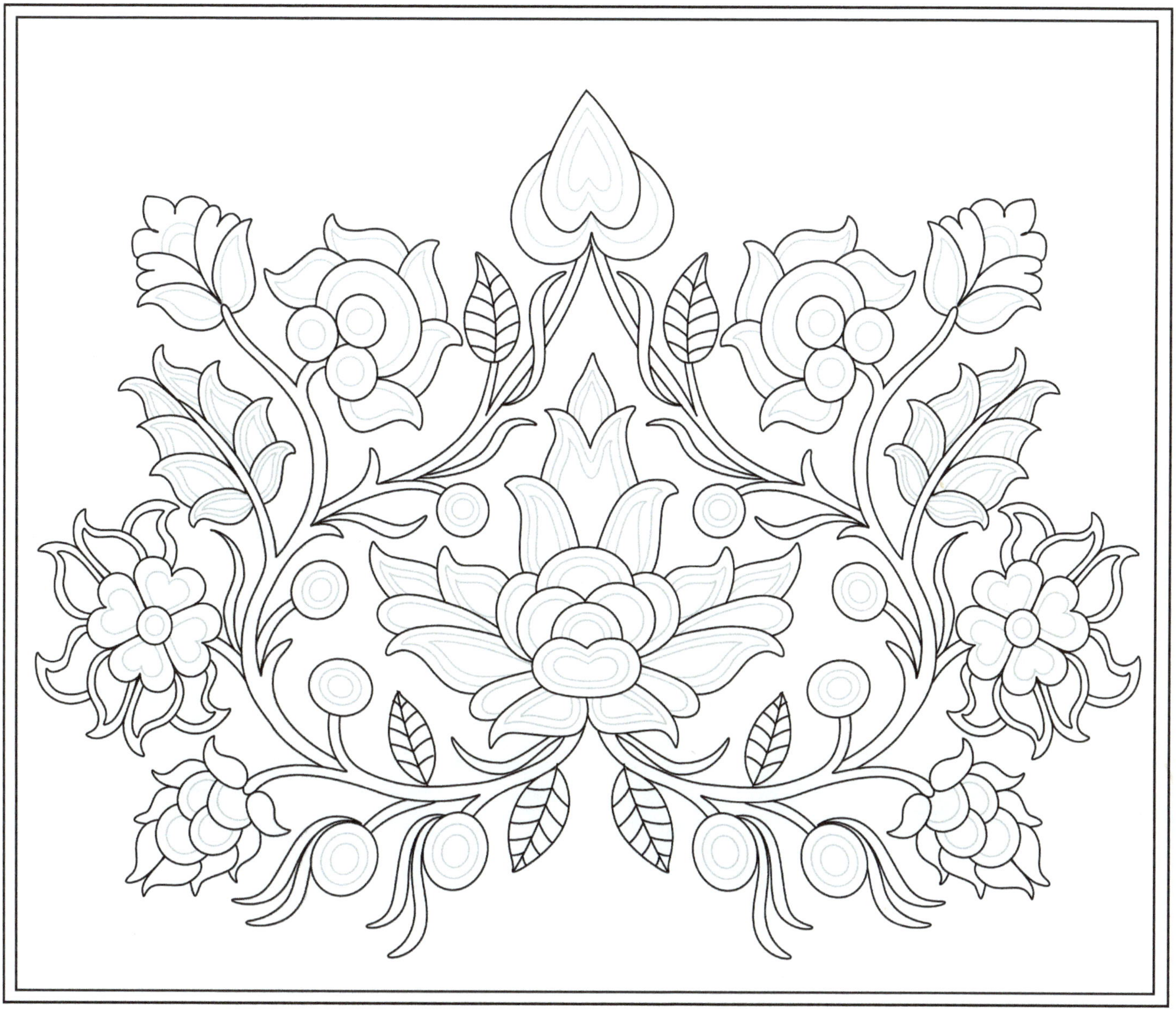

Color the drawing above using your preferred choice of colors.

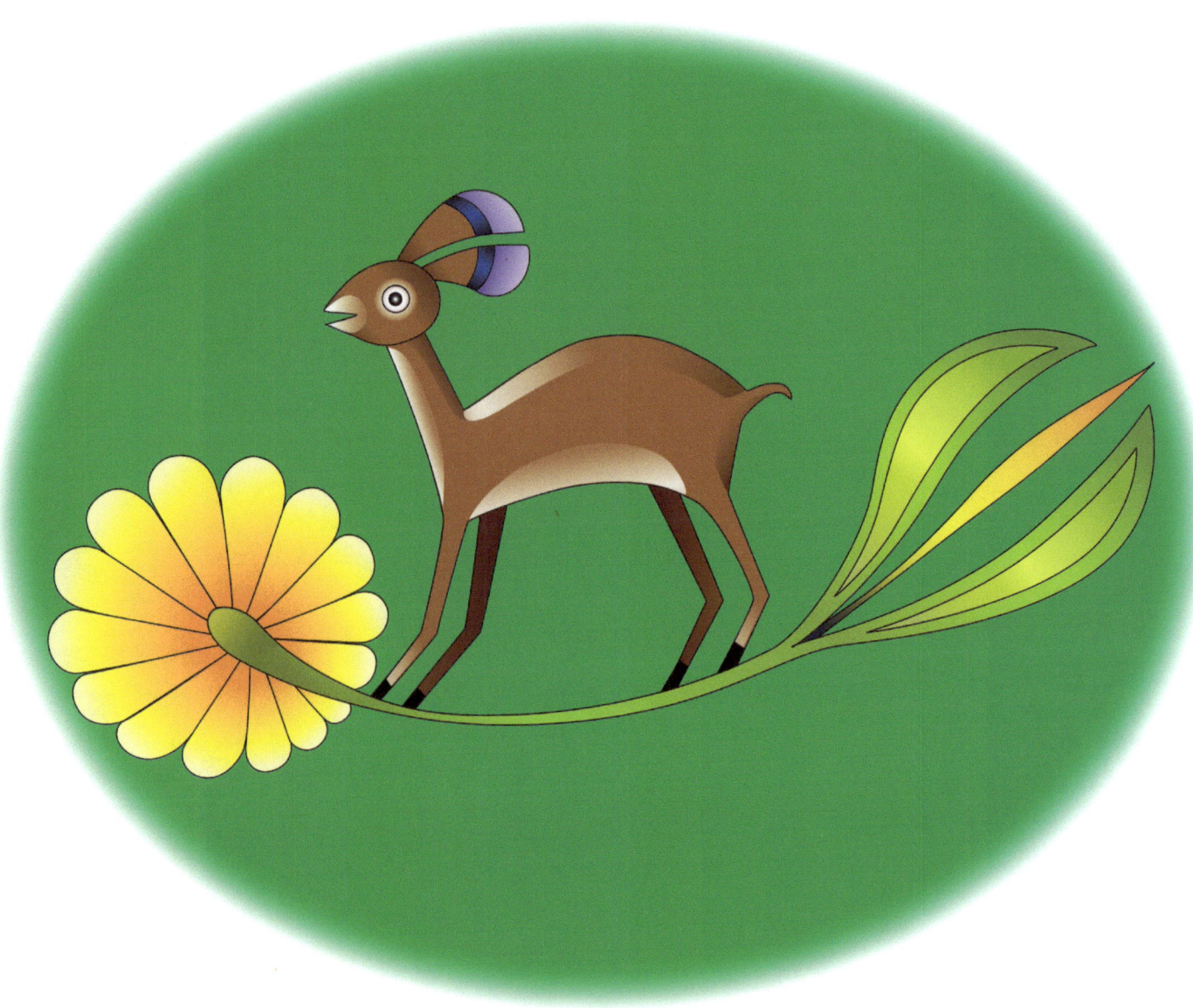

This object of extraordinary beauty was produced by Hopi jewelers.
Hopis lived in Arizona and New Mexico.

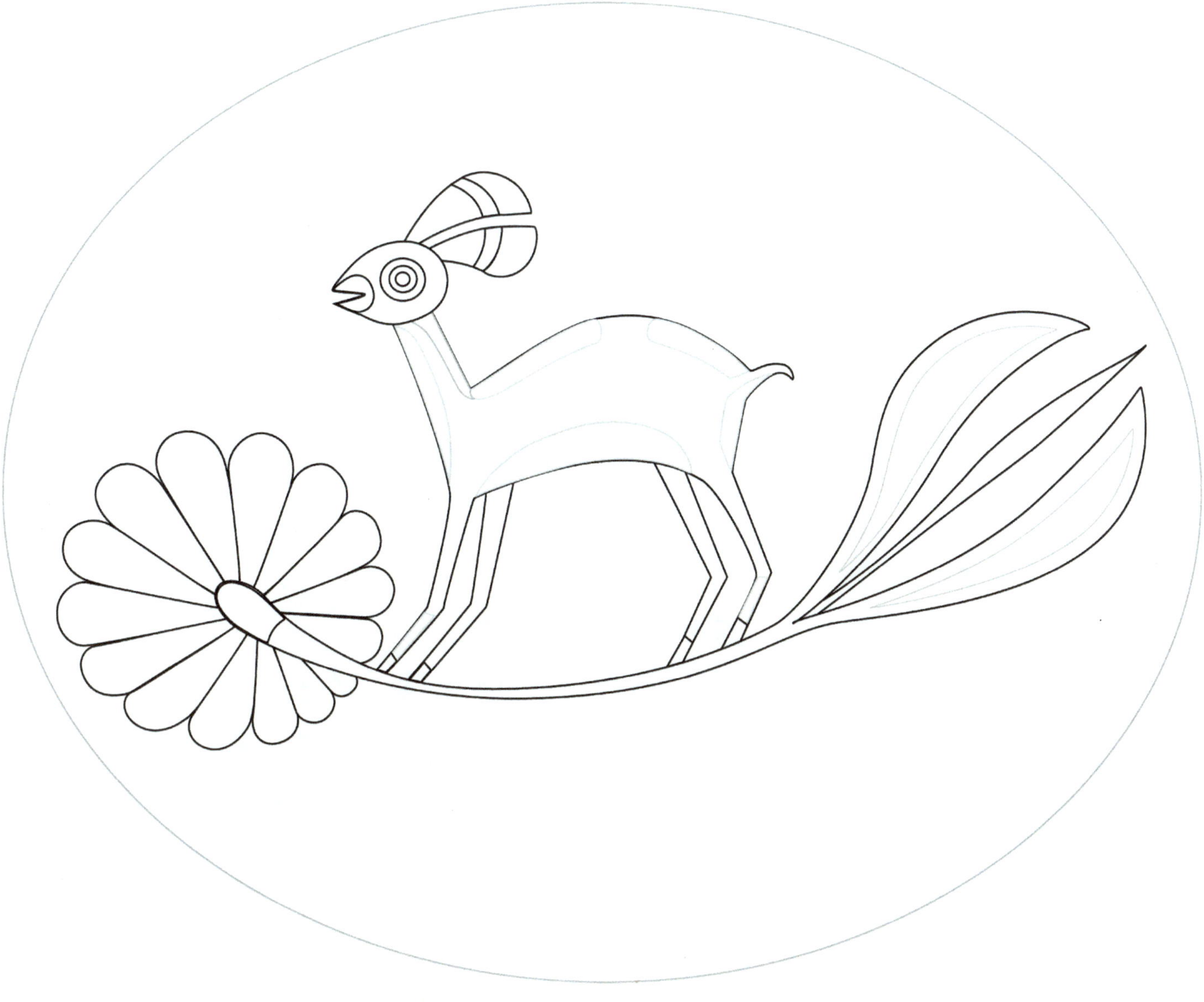

Color the drawing above using your preferred choice of colors.

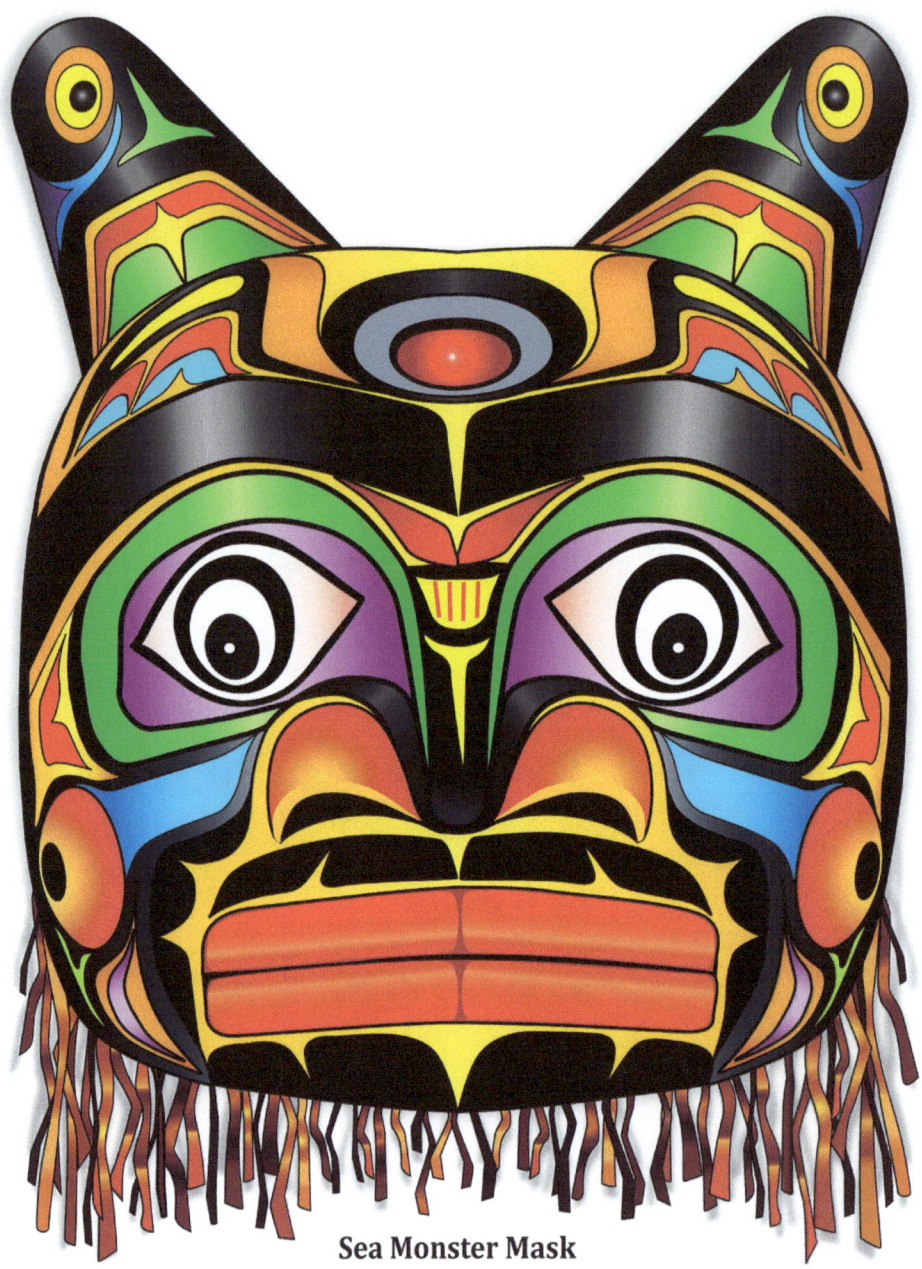

Sea Monster Mask

The mask represents a specific sea monster who came out of the sea to build a house, assisted by a Thunderbird, Western Canada.

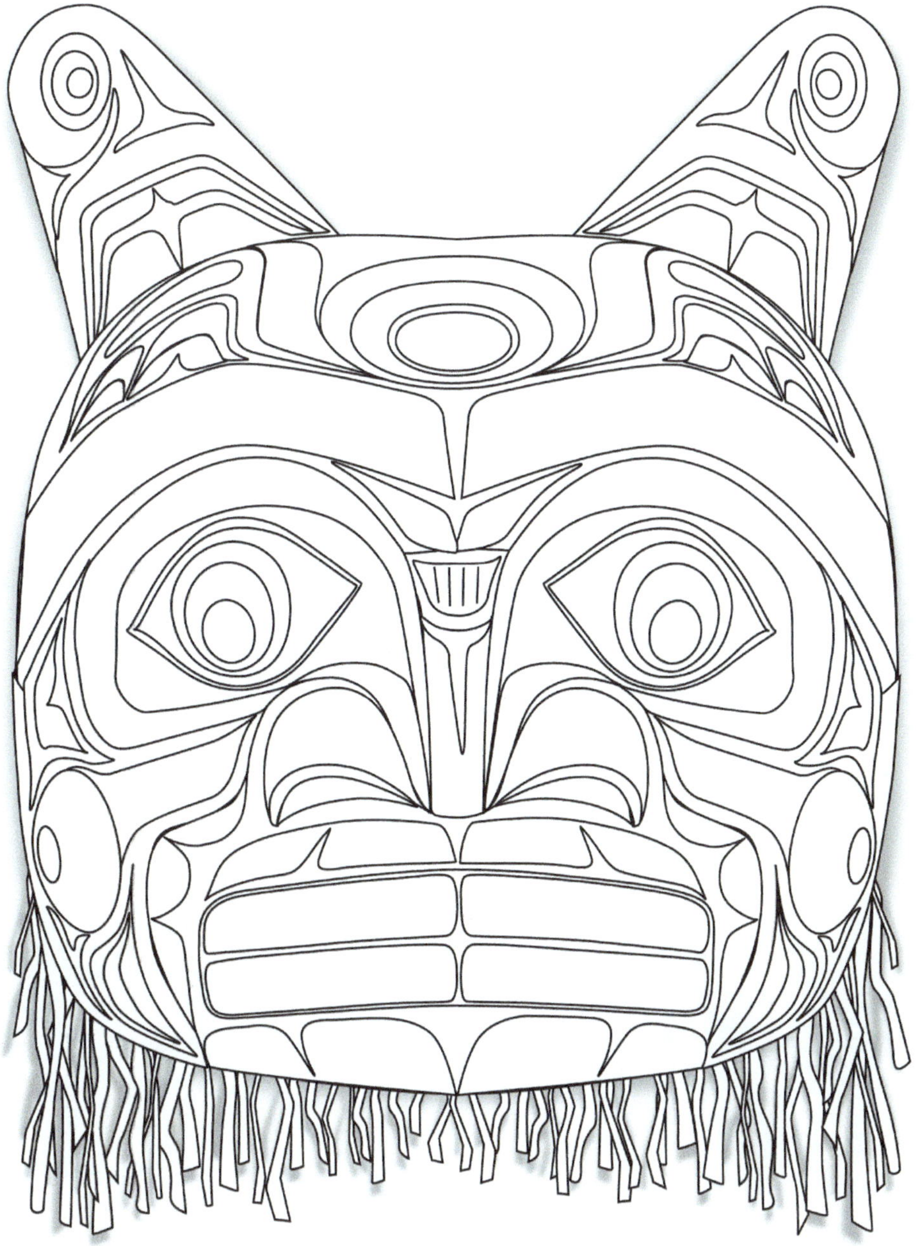

Color the drawing above using your preferred choice of colors.

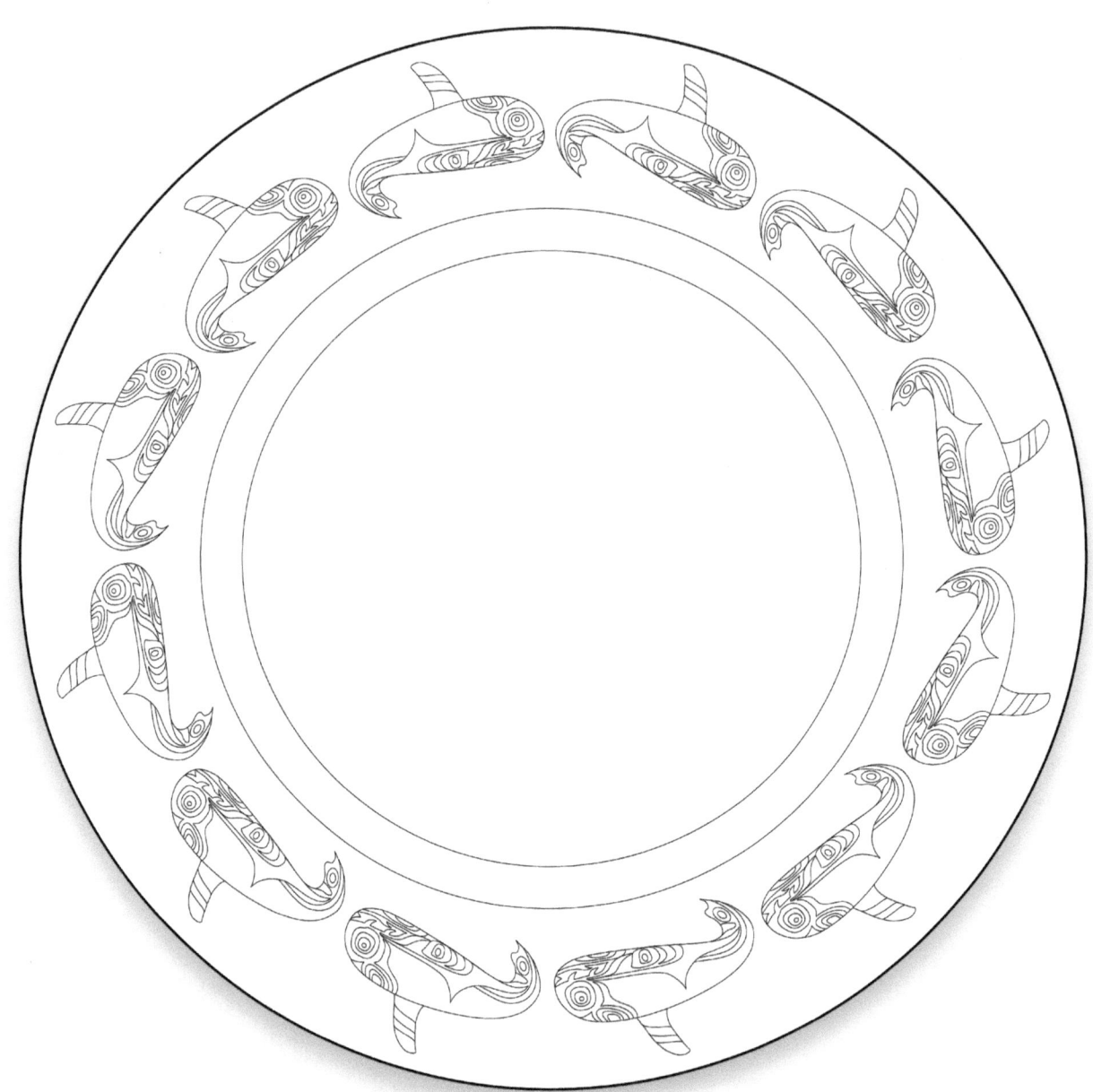

Using these images as examples, create your own piece using the elements found in American Indian Art.

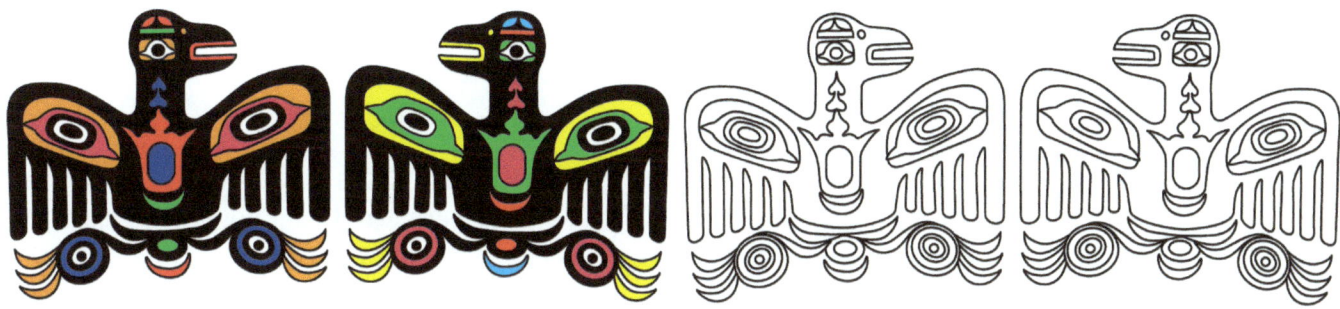

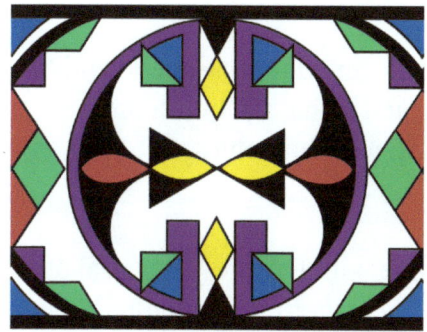

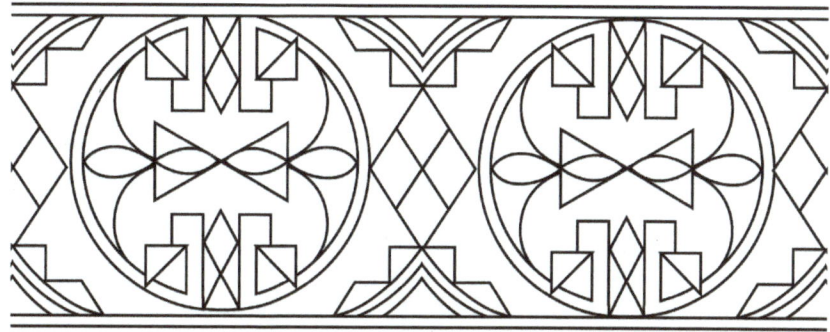

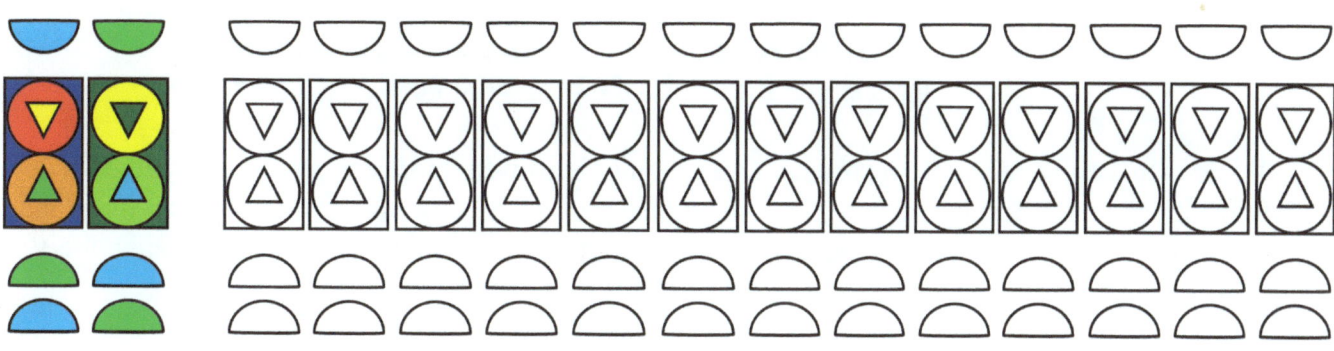

Color the drawings above using your preferred choice of colors.

= a synopsis of =
American Indian art

Indigenous Art or more commonly known as North American Indian Art is astonishingly diverse containing forms of art, created by the original inhabitants of North America and their cognate descendants. It carries several different cultures within the category and spans a great time sequence ranging from prehistoric era to present time. North American First Nations art has been divided into five major regions of the continent: The South, The East, The West, The Northwest Coast, and The North. The role of the artists has been to arouse an emotional response from the audience. Their art encompassed the sacred, the secular, ceremonial, commercial, political, and even the domestic.

The surviving artifacts demonstrate that the ancient man had a considerable amount of aesthetic ability. The artists skillfully produced well-balanced forms in both pottery and stone carvings alike. Originally the color was achieved from mineral pigments and vegetable dyes, and later supplemented by commercial dyes and trade colors.

The Native tradition did not necessarily establish an object's relative value with its purely material and visual features. The visual pleasure from a Cree woman's bitten birch-bark pattern is the reality of her inner vision. In the North, Yupik artists depicted mystical journeys of Shamans in carved and painted masks. In the Northwest Coast, masks were exhibited in potlatches which represented the wearers' inherited powers and prerogatives about the location of the political power. Iroquois, in the Northwest, are famous for making False Face Society masks, Quillwork, Beadwork, and Wooden bowls. The Haidas brilliantly crafted the Crest and Totem poles as memorials, that can reach a height of 60 feet or more.

While men's art were mainly representational, women's art were more commonly abstract. Men traditionally carved ritual pipes and masks, and women created artwork associated with clay, fiber, and basketry. The Pueblo women in the New Mexico region have crafted outstanding baskets and pottery.

New York Abstract Expressionists like Jackson Pollock (1912-1956), Barnett Newman (1905-1970), and the Canadian Group of Seven members have grounded their art in the traditional indigenous art of North America.

OTHER TITLES IN THIS SERIES

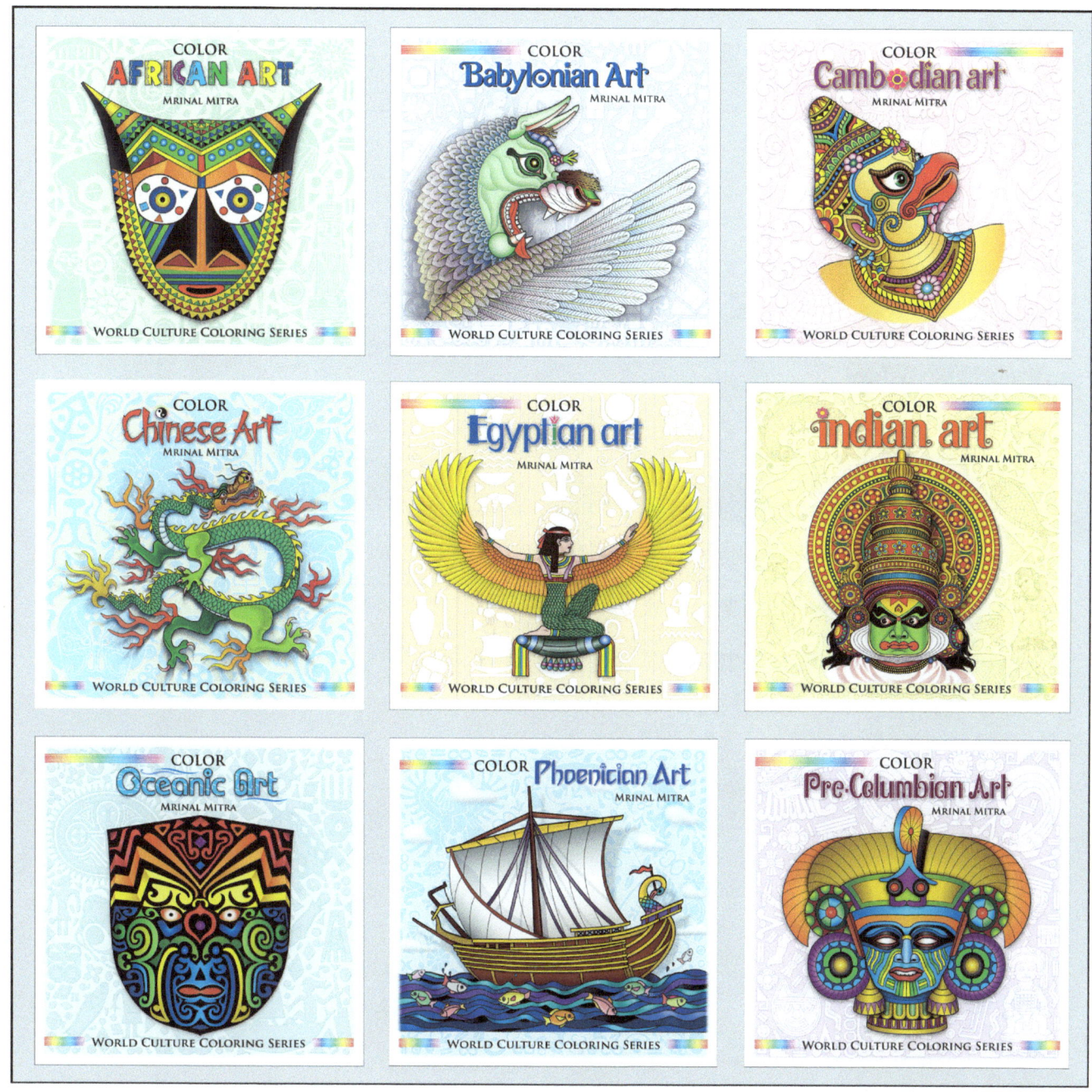

COLOR
AFRICAN ART
MRINAL MITRA
WORLD CULTURE COLORING SERIES

COLOR
Babylonian Art
MRINAL MITRA
WORLD CULTURE COLORING SERIES

COLOR
Cambodian art
MRINAL MITRA
WORLD CULTURE COLORING SERIES

COLOR
Chinese Art
MRINAL MITRA
WORLD CULTURE COLORING SERIES

COLOR
Egyptian art
MRINAL MITRA
WORLD CULTURE COLORING SERIES

COLOR
indian art
MRINAL MITRA
WORLD CULTURE COLORING SERIES

COLOR
Oceanic Art
MRINAL MITRA
WORLD CULTURE COLORING SERIES

COLOR **Phoenician Art**
MRINAL MITRA
WORLD CULTURE COLORING SERIES

COLOR
Pre-Columbian Art
MRINAL MITRA
WORLD CULTURE COLORING SERIES

AVAILABLE FROM AMAZON.COM, CREATESPACE.COM, AND OTHER RETAIL OUTLETS

Acknowledgement

First and foremost, this series would not be possible without the number of great historical art found within the different cultural regions around the world.

In addition, we would like to acknowledge the variety of publishing's from all over the world for allowing us to learn about their fascinating ancestral art and culture. With this provided knowledge, we have hoped to have represented the art as splendidly as you have supplied it.

About the Author

Mrinal Mitra has earned a number of prestigious awards, both Indian and International, and received honors for his outstanding illustrations. Some of his recognitions include; The Noma Concours Award, Japan (twice), Illustrators Award, and Children's Choice Award, India, and honors from German Television "Transtel", BRNO- CSSR, TIBI- Iran, and UNICEF, New York.

Many of his talented artworks have been exhibited in several different countries such as; India, Japan, Italy, Czech Republic, Iran, and New Zealand. Mitra has authored, designed and illustrated trade and educational children's books for many Indian as well as Multinational Book Publishers around the globe.

Copyright: Mrinal Mitra, 2014

Printed by CreateSpace, An Amazon.com. Company
Available from Amazon.com, CreateSpace.com, and other retail outlets

For further inquiry please contact Mrinal Mitra at: mitra_mrinal@hotmail.com